Our Time

Our Time

Breaking the Silence of
"Don't Ask, Don't Tell"

JOSH SEEFRIED

THE PENGUIN PRESS

New York

2011

THE PENGUIN PRESS
Published by the Penguin Group
Penguin Group (USA) Inc., 375 Hudson Street, New York, New York 10014, U.S.A. • Penguin Group
(Canada), 90 Eglinton Avenue East, Suite 700, Toronto, Ontario, Canada M4P 2Y3 (a division of
Pearson Penguin Canada Inc.) • Penguin Books Ltd, 80 Strand, London WC2R 0RL, England • Penguin
Ireland, 25 St. Stephen's Green, Dublin 2, Ireland (a division of Penguin Books Ltd) • Penguin Books
Australia Ltd, 250 Camberwell Road, Camberwell, Victoria 3124, Australia (a division of
Pearson Australia Group Pty Ltd) • Penguin Books India Pvt Ltd, 11 Community Centre, Panchsheel
Park, New Delhi – 110 017, India • Penguin Group (NZ), 67 Apollo Drive, Rosedale, Auckland 0632,
New Zealand (a division of Pearson New Zealand Ltd) • Penguin Books (South Africa) (Pty) Ltd,
24 Sturdee Avenue, Rosebank, Johannesburg 2196, South Africa

Penguin Books Ltd, Registered Offices: 80 Strand, London WC2R 0RL, England

First published in 2011 by The Penguin Press, a member of Penguin Group (USA) Inc.

Copyright © Joshua David Seefried, 2011
All rights reserved

The selections in this book are the copyrighted properties of the respective
authors and are published by arrangement with the rights owners.

ISBN 978-1-59420-331-2

Printed in the United States of America
1   3   5   7   9   10   8   6   4   2

DESIGNED BY AMANDA DEWEY

To all the gay, lesbian, bisexual,
and transgender service members
who have given their lives
for this great nation

AUTHOR'S NOTE

I asked contributors to share their stories after President Obama signed "Don't Ask, Don't Tell" legislation on December 22, 2010, but before the repeal became final on September 20, 2011. Because of the uncertainty during this interim period, some contributors chose to be identified by a pseudonym. Some contributors also chose to protect the identity of those they mentioned by using a pseudonym. All pseudonyms are identified by an asterisk after the name the first time the name appears.

The stories reflect the opinions of individual service members and those opinions do not necessarily reflect the opinions of their branches of service or of the Department of Defense.

PREFACE

Patrick Murphy

Patrick Murphy led the fight to repeal "Don't Ask, Don't Tell." He was America's first Iraq war veteran to serve in the U.S. Congress and represented Pennsylvania's 8th Congressional District, serving from 2007 to 2011. Captain Murphy earned the Bronze Star for service in the Iraq War as a paratrooper in the 82nd Airborne Division.

For seventeen years, a cruel irony hung over the debate on "Don't Ask, Don't Tell." While politicians and talking heads offered a flurry of opinions on the issue, one important contingency could not participate in the discussion: the men and women whose lives hung in the balance. Because they could not serve openly, they also could not defend their right to openly serve the nation they loved.

In *Our Time,* the silence is finally broken and we hear the voices of the gay and lesbian service members who have borne this exceptional burden. We learn new truths from those most affected by DADT and gain perspective on the unjust policy.

As someone who served our country in combat and understands the pride and responsibility that comes from wearing our uniform, these stories resonate with me. The constant fear of investigation, the agonizing over who you can trust, and the pain of isolation were all familiar. Also familiar were the stories of tolerance, of soldiers who value their comrades on their performance alone.

Remarkable acts of courage are found throughout *Our Time.* In one account, a gay drill sergeant sees a gay recruit harassed by other drill instructors. The recruit struggles and ultimately attempts suicide. The drill sergeant resolves never to let that happen again and becomes a resource for gay recruits who might be at risk, inspiring and counseling them. He courageously risks his own career to help them succeed and serve our nation.

In another account, a soldier explains what it's like to serve in Iraq when no one can know about your loved one at home. He needs to constantly police his language and mail, and is terrified that he might be betrayed and found out. The notion that a man is putting his life on the line for his country, but still has to hide his loved ones, is unconscionable to me as an American. Every person who puts on a military uniform to serve should be able to reach out to his or her family—including his or her partner—without fear. That's why we worked so hard to finally end DADT.

Those of us who have been fortunate enough to lead troops never lose our love for our fellow soldiers, nor do we ever stop being thankful for their service. We owe our gratitude to the men and women who fight to defend our nation. Anyone who shares that appreciation for the bravery of our troops should read the stories of these young men and women who embody the best of our military values: honor, courage, and selfless sacrifice. They remind us why every man or woman who wants to serve our nation should have the opportunity to do so and why these heroes deserve the thanks of a grateful nation.

Our Time

INTRODUCTION

President Barack Obama signed the "Don't Ask, Don't Tell" Repeal Act bill into law on December 22, 2010. Though it would be a few months until repeal took effect, that day marked the beginning of a new era for the American military. I sat in the audience during the signing ceremony that day as a representative of OutServe and as an active duty gay Air Force officer directly affected by the policy. It was thrilling to celebrate this hard victory alongside other advocates, but I also knew that despite the leap forward there remained a tremendous amount of work to be done. For seventeen years, the policy had effectively silenced an entire military population. The ways in which "Don't Ask, Don't Tell" had poisoned military culture remained untold.

I knew the negative effects of this silence firsthand. As a brand new officer at training school, I was blackmailed by an instructor who knew my orientation, but under "Don't Ask, Don't Tell" I had no real outlet to stop this abuse. It was this experience that pushed me to found OutServe, along with one of my closest civilian friends, Ty Walrod. The organization began small. In November 2009 my friends and colleagues, outraged by what had happened to me, formed a Facebook group and website titled "Citizens for Repeal of 'Don't Ask, Don't Tell.'" Soon the page was gaining hundreds of followers daily. I knew that there were thousands of active duty LGBT service members who would benefit from having a support network, but this was proof. We moved quickly to create an underground social networking site for active duty LGBT service members. Until the formation of OutServe, there had been no safe way to create an organized LGBT community in the military. The risk of exposure was far too great. By providing identity security we were able to create a safe space where active duty military personnel could openly form friendships and voice concerns. To date, OutServe has successfully connected more than 4,000 LGBT military personnel around the world.

Our Time is our story of our military experience under "Don't Ask, Don't Tell." The individuals you will meet in these pages served in silence. They were required to withhold an integral part of themselves from their colleagues. They could not freely share their love for their families or their dreams for the future. They had no protection when individuals used the "Don't Ask, Don't Tell" policy to blackmail and harass. However, as active duty service members themselves know, the silence of "Don't Ask, Don't Tell" was already beginning to break. The stories here are testament to the remarkable friendships that form between soldiers, relationships of respect and affection that transcend prejudice and prove just how very outdated and bankrupt the "Don't Ask, Don't Tell" policy was.

Throughout *Our Time*, you will note time and time again one word: "integrity." This concept is a cornerstone of military education and tradition; it is a value we are taught to aspire to and to uphold. And yet "Don't Ask, Don't Tell" denied integrity to each and every LGBT service member. Every day these individuals were faced with a deep, wounding conflict: to be true to themselves or true to their country. The pain of that choice is felt in almost every story included here.

I reached out to contributors during the period after the repeal act was signed, but before "Don't Ask, Don't Tell" had officially ended. Sharing their stories during this uncertain moment was an act of bravery, and I thank each contributor for his or her work toward helping those outside the military understand just how damaging and far-reaching the effects of "Don't Ask, Don't Tell" were. Their courage in service of this book, however, is nothing compared to the courage and self-sacrifice our country required of every LGBT soldier who served under "Don't Ask, Don't Tell." I also want to give special thanks to the straight active duty and family members who shared their experiences, and to the military personnel who served during the early years of the policy. Their words remind us of how far we have come.

Looking forward, there are new challenges we must confront. Many foreign militaries have long allowed gay service members to serve openly, yet many are still afraid to come out of the closet. In order to ensure that does not happen here in America, gay troops must lead. This means creating a visible, respectful LGBT military community. There are battles left to fight. Our marriages are still not recognized by the government and military families will be torn apart because they cannot seek joint military assignments. We must also not forget our transgender brothers and sisters who still cannot serve openly.

When service members sent me their stories, they would often thank me for the opportunity to contribute. They told me that there was a certain vindication in writing their story on paper and knowing it was going to be read. The human narrative is a powerful tool. It was the courage of previous gay service members' stories that motivated the nation to change this policy and it's these stories that will help the pain of the last few decades of discrimination heal.

One story in particular speaks to the spirit of unity and trust within the military. On February 27, 2011, Corporal Andrew Wilfahrt, a gay soldier, was killed by a roadside bomb while serving in Afghanistan. Lori and Jeff Wilfahrt, Andrew's parents, had the courage to share the story of their son and how he was treated in his unit. His mother proudly stated everyone in his unit knew he was gay and nobody cared. Andrew's father later shared a letter with me that he had received from his son's Army unit still deployed in Afghanistan. Andrew's comrades decided to name their combat outpost after him. Those soldiers didn't need months of training or a PowerPoint presentation to learn respect of their fallen gay comrade. They respected Andrew because he had their back. Corporal Wilfahrt's unit embodies the very best of military culture.

These soldiers are an example for service in the post-"Don't Ask, Don't Tell" military. They are a reminder that respect and professionalism is already a part of our culture. What we need now is leadership. Gay service members must lead from the front openly and straight colleagues must help create an atmosphere of acceptance and respect. This is the message that the men and women who contributed to this book are sending with their stories. It's now our time.

—Josh Seefried

No matter how I look at the issue . . . I cannot escape being troubled by the fact that we have in place a policy which forces young men and women to lie about who they are in order to defend their fellow citizens. . . . For me, it comes down to integrity—theirs as individuals and ours as an institution."

—Chairman of the Joint Chiefs of Staff Admiral Michael Mullen,
at the Senate Armed Services Committee
"Don't Ask, Don't Tell" hearing

Jim Cauthen is a staff sergeant and aircraft
metals technologist in the U.S. Air Force. He has
deployed multiple times and is currently stationed
at Mountain Home Air Force Base, Idaho.

I came out to my parents when I was sixteen. It didn't go over too well. My father made it perfectly clear that I was no longer his son. The shame of having a homosexual child couldn't be brought upon his household. Long lectures soon followed in hopes to scare the "gay" out of me. Deep inside I felt I needed to get away from this influence and I made the decision to join the military as soon as I could. Slowly I started to pull away from my family, not letting my parents or two sisters know anything about my personal life, as it was the only way I could avoid the lectures, the glares, the tangible hate.

I enlisted in the United States Air Force, and a year after basic training was stationed at my first base, at Mountain Home Air Force Base, Idaho. As I learned the mechanics of all the different aircraft, I also learned a lot about myself and gained a sense of pride knowing I was doing something that made such an impact.

After almost two years without contact with my family, I slowly started reopening communications with them. My mother was my main contact, and sometimes my sisters. They would tell me, "Dad says hi." I'd ignore that little part and continue the conversation. We made plans for the family to come visit in 1999 for an air show that was to be hosted at my base. I was excited and scared. Owen, my roommate at the time, knew I was apprehensive, but he didn't know the full story of how or why I had ended my relationship with my family. I had come out to him by accident only a few months prior, and luckily it didn't hurt our friendship. If anything, it made it stronger. He talked about his girlfriends like he always did, and we joked about guys and friends of ours that I found attractive.

The air show was canceled, but the plans for the visit didn't change. My family wanted to see where I was living, how I was doing. I wanted to show them that I had become someone they would be proud to call their son. They arrived in town and I met them for a nice dinner that night. It was almost like nothing had ever happened. We shared stories of life over the last few years, enjoying the feeling of being a family again. The next day I showed them around the base. They had the chance to see the aircraft from a distance, I showed them the dorms and introduced them to Owen, and we explored the small town of Mountain Home. As I dropped them off at their hotel that evening, we made plans for the next day.

As my mom and sisters got out of my truck and closed the doors, my father stayed in the front seat and laid into me with his most hateful lecture to date. Two years of pent-up frustration, shame, and hate let loose like a broken dam. Using his interpretation of the Bible, he quoted Scriptures and made sure I *knew* I was going to hell. He made sure I knew I was an abomination, that I was sinful in God's eyes. Memories from years before flooded back as I sat there in the driver's seat listening to him. The excitement and love I'd felt the whole day and the evening before suddenly vanished. I was a kid again, waiting to be punished. All I had worked for over those last few years was for nothing. I'd failed at making him proud. After what felt like an eternity, he stopped. I took a deep breath. I got my bearings and asked if he was done, then asked him to get out of my truck. As soon as the door closed, I started the truck and made my way back to the base, ten miles away.

I cried the entire drive back to the base, not focusing on or caring about anything around me. I remember having thoughts of what it would be like to hit a telephone pole or another car head-on while doing eighty on the sixty-miles-per-hour road that led back to the base. To this day I don't remember how I made it through the front gate. When I got back to the dorms and into my room, I slammed the door and screamed in frustration, anger, pain.

My roommate walked over to the door and just stood there—he

knew I wasn't okay, so he didn't ask. With a shaking hand, I held out my keys and cell phone, and asked him not to give them to me for the next few days. He pocketed them and just kept looking at me. He didn't say anything, but guided me over to the couch in our room. I just stood there, and he motioned me to sit down. I refused. He stepped up to me and wrapped his arms around me. One arm wrapped around my back and the other around my head. He pulled me in tight and didn't let me go. It was too much for me and I started sobbing in his arms. He held me tight as I shook. He didn't say anything, didn't ask. He didn't need to.

In that hour, Owen saved my life. He held me, a broken man, in his arms and quietly waited for my will to live to flow back into me. This one man, who didn't see a wretched, sinful abomination before him, pulled me back from the edge. He made sure I made it through the night. He didn't care that I was gay. He cared that I was hurt. He cared that something had pushed me that far. I can never repay him for that night. But to this day, I remember what it was like to feel total, unconditional love from another person.

Dr. Jamey Burton is a physician of family medicine and was a flight surgeon while in the Army. She currently resides in New York with her wife, Lisa, and they are expecting the arrival of their first child next spring.

"Are you ready to be a civilian now?" the clerk in the transitions office asked me as I signed my DD 214 form releasing me from active duty on October 7, 2010.

A rapid flurry of thoughts and emotions passed through me: anger—I wasn't ready to give up my Army career because of an archaic law; frustration—because our military leaders could not see how immaterial being gay is to being a good soldier or physician; fear—because I didn't know what lay ahead for me; guilt—for leaving my dedicated comrades, coworkers, and patients behind; relief—that I could now live honestly and openly with my wife; excitement—that I would no longer be treated as a prisoner because of who I am; and optimism—that I could tell my story and inspire others to keep fighting the good fight.

I enlisted in the National Guard at seventeen, both because I needed a way to pay for college and because I had a deep, burning urge to serve a purpose greater than myself. I attended West Point, where I graduated with honors and was part of the 2 percent selected to attend medical school directly after graduation. I chose to attend the Uniformed Services University of the Health Sciences, or USU, and was awarded the Army Surgeon General's Award upon graduation. I completed my residency in family medicine, earning both an Army Achievement Medal and an Army Commendation Medal my graduating year. Before PCS'ing—receiving a permanent change of station—I married my partner, Lisa, in Massachusetts, and we had a beautiful ceremony at our church in North Carolina, where I was stationed.

Later, when I attended the Officer Career Course, one of the speakers said something that resonated with me. "Each one of you are challenged on your Army values each and every day," he said, and went on to emphasize the importance of integrity, leadership, and trust as an Army physician. It was there that the seed was planted: *I am living a lie. I'm lying to my patients. I am a lie. Can I do this for another fifteen years?* This struck me to the core. How could I force my wife to stay in hiding for another fifteen years? How were we to have children, then raise them to lie about their mom—"Don't out Mommy now, okay?" How would it be to PCS to different states that didn't recognize us? What would happen if I got stationed overseas and my wife couldn't obtain a visa to go with me? We wanted our love, our lives, and our family to grow, but staying in the Army wouldn't allow that.

It was only a matter of time, I feared, before one of my patients figured me out and reported me. There was much debate, and I both met with JAG—the "judge advocates" who give legal advice in the military—and spoke with a legal adviser from the Servicemembers Legal Defense Network (SLDN), an advocacy group for gays and lesbians in the military. A few months later, I chose to write a statement sharing my thoughts and feelings about the difficulties of living as a gay soldier, wife, and physician. I did not say I wanted to be discharged. I did not say I wanted to leave the Army. I, along with many of my superiors and colleagues, figured that with the high operations speed of today's Army and deployments, my career field, which was so essential to the armed services, and with ten and a half years still remaining of my active duty obligation, they would simply retain me and wait out the DADT litigation in the courts and the legislation working its way through Congress. I was wrong. To the Army, it was more important that I had married the woman I loved than that I saved lives on the battlefield.

My coworkers, colleagues, and patients alike were shocked I was being "eliminated." Even worse was the heading on my discharge/elimination memorandum:

MEMORANDUM FOR Commander, U.S. Army Human Resources Command–Alexandria

SUBJECT: Resignation for the Good of the Service due to Homosexual Conduct Case
(BROWN, Jamey A., ██████████, CPT, RA, MC)

How so very untrue this was. Not simply for me, but for thousands of soldiers, sailors, airmen, and Marines who have risked their lives—some paying the ultimate sacrifice—to be discharged for "*the good of the service.*"

Most, if not all, of my coworkers and colleagues knew I was gay, yet I was never ostracized. My colleagues at the clinic were unwaveringly supportive throughout my entire discharge process—from the time I came out until my last day in the office. Words cannot express the gratitude I have for them. Ironically, it was my last day in the Army that the military, in its way, recognized my marriage— by listing my wife as my nearest relative and spouse on my DD 214, forever emblazoning it in my military record.

The information contained herein is subject to computer matching within the Department of Defense or with any other affected Federal or non-Federal agency for verification purposes and to determine eligibility for, and/or continued compliance with, the requirements of a Federal benefit program.		
19a. MAILING ADDRESS AFTER SEPARATION *(Include ZIP Code)*	**b. NEAREST RELATIVE** *(Name and address - Include ZIP Code)* LISA ▇▇▇ (SPOUSE)	
NEW YORK ▇▇▇	NEW YORK ▇▇▇	
20. MEMBER REQUESTS COPY 6 BE SENT TO *(Specify state/locality)* NY	OFFICE OF VETERANS AFFAIRS	X YES NO
a. MEMBER REQUESTS COPY 3 BE SENT TO THE CENTRAL OFFICE OF THE DEPARTMENT OF VETERANS AFFAIRS (WASHINGTON, DC)		X YES NO
21.a. MEMBER SIGNATURE SIGNED BY: BROWN.JAMEY.ANN.1074598400	**b. DATE** *(YYYYMMDD)* 20101007	**22.a. OFFICIAL AUTHORIZED TO SIGN** *(Typed name, grade, title, signature)* SIGNED BY: DEROUIN.NANCY.M.1269847782 **b. DATE** *(YYYYMMDD)* 20101007 NANCY DEROUIN, SERCO LEAD

SPECIAL ADDITIONAL INFORMATION *(For use by authorized agencies only)*		
23. TYPE OF SEPARATION DISCHARGE	**24. CHARACTER OF SERVICE** *(Include upgrades)* HONORABLE	
25. SEPARATION AUTHORITY AR 600-8-24, PARA 4-22	**26. SEPARATION CODE** JRC	**27. REENTRY CODE** NA
28. NARRATIVE REASON FOR SEPARATION HOMOSEXUAL CONDUCT (MARRIAGE OR ATTEMPTED MARRIAGE)		
29. DATES OF TIME LOST DURING THIS PERIOD *(YYYYMMDD)* NONE		**30. MEMBER REQUESTS COPY 4** *(Initials)* JAB

DD FORM 214, AUG 2009   PREVIOUS EDITION IS OBSOLETE. GENERATED BY TRANSPROC   **MEMBER - 4**

Jonathan Mills is a staff sergeant and electronic technician for the U.S. Air Force currently stationed in Washington, D.C. He is the first executive editor of **OutServe Magazine.**

I can still remember the exact moment when I knew, beyond a shadow of a doubt, that my U.S. Air Force career had come to an end. I had made a valiant effort at hiding my sexuality from my employer (and myself) for four years, but now the truth was about to set me free . . . of a job. My mind was racing a mile a minute, and I could feel my pulse blasting through my body.

Four years earlier I had married my high school sweetheart. We were very much in love, but that doesn't mean I wasn't conflicted. As the son of a fundamentalist Baptist preacher, I was raised in an über-conservative household. When I did finally work up the courage to come out to my parents during my senior year in high school, I was promptly sent to a Christian counselor to try out a little "reparative therapy." These sessions weren't cheap and my family was not wealthy, so in an effort to make it easier on my parents, who were obviously heartbroken and humiliated, I decided I was "fixed" and quit going. I'd be lying, though, if I said I didn't actually believe the counselor. I thought I could be fixed: God didn't want me to be that way, and all I had to do was resist the temptation, and eventually, with God's help, it would just go away.

So in an effort to prove that I had "healed," and because I truly did care very much about my then girlfriend, we got married. I joined the Air Force the next week. Fresh out of basic training and newly married, I was confident, hopeful, and naive. The next four years proved to be much harder than I had ever anticipated. Trying to keep my feelings bottled up inside me, trying to figure out what those feelings even were, trying to keep my wife emotionally and physically satisfied—it all took a huge toll on me and erupted several times over the course of our marriage in a volcanic burst of shouting, threats, and tears.

Eventually it became too much. I found myself sitting at my desk one Friday night, working a late shift, and asking myself: *What the hell am I doing? How long can I keep this up? What's the point, when it can only end one way?* I felt trapped, desperate, and lonely. I made an appointment with a military chaplain for the following Monday. The next morning, my wife and I had another argument and I laid it all out on the table. I told her I had been fighting being gay for my whole life and I was tired of it—I couldn't do it one day longer. It was selfish for me to expect her to stay in a marriage that could not provide her what she needed, and it was naive for me to think I could keep my sanity and well-being intact for even one more year under the current circumstances. More important than anything else, though, was the fact that continuing to deny who I was not only made me selfish, it also made me a coward and a liar. The aftermath of my heart-to-heart with my wife was, in some ways, worse than the actual moment of truth itself. In a testament to her character and maturity, she empathized with me up to a point—after all, I had confided to her my feelings toward guys long before we were even married; she had just believed the same thing I did, that being attracted to guys was something you could just get over. We spent the next few days talking and deciding where to go from there. One night we were out getting coffee at our favorite coffee shop, in Italy, where we lived at the time, and we just started crying, right in front of a café full of extremely curious and slightly alarmed Italians. We cared about each other very much, but there was no hope for our marriage. We knew we had finally come face-to-face with the truth, and liberating though it was, it was also very ugly and painful.

That Monday, I called my supervisor to ask him if I could have the day off to take care of some personal business—we were going to use the day to discuss our separation and make arrangements for her moving back to the U.S. He asked me to come into work and talk with him before I did anything else. I immediately panicked, because I did not see how I could possibly be honest with him about why we were separating—and he *would* get it out of me anyway, because I wouldn't be able to lie to him. Still, I pulled on my uniform and climbed into my car, driving as slowly as I could possibly go without angering the Italians behind me. As predicted, when I got to work, my boss started in with, "Tell me what is *really* going on." We got into his car and drove around the base for a while, he trying to give me effective marriage counseling, I trying to skirt his questions and be as vague as humanly possible. I tried to repeatedly convey to him the severity of our situation, but it was hard to convey how troubled my marriage was without coming out to him.

Finally, he told me we were going to drive to my house to talk with my wife and me about it together, just to make absolutely certain we both knew exactly what we were doing. My heart jumped to my throat and my breakfast threatened to follow. The whole ride there I prayed that his car would somehow go off the road and crash into a tree. Alas, he did not lose control of the vehicle. We made it almost all the way to my house before I worked up the courage to take control of the situation. I told him to stop the car and swallowed back the breakfast that was making good on its threat of a midmorning reappearance.

We sat in silence while he looked at me and I looked down at my feet, as if the right words would just materialize there on the floor mats. For what seemed like hours but was actually just minutes, my heart pounded in my ears and my hands sweat and shook. This was the moment where my short-lived Air Force career would officially come to a screeching halt. And then I just said it: "I want to be honest with you and I know I can trust you. We are getting separated because I'm gay."

His gaze did not shift. He kept looking at me as if to say, "Come again?" What seemed like another eternity elapsed until he said, "Oh."

I don't remember what either of us said immediately after that, but he still wanted to talk to my wife and me—to make sure we were both okay. Once we were at my house, just before walking in he turned to me and said, "Jonathan, it's okay. It's going to be all right."

His simple assurance spared my career and reassured me that my supervisor was a man of principle—a man just like Admiral Mullen, who testified before Congress that repealing DADT was simply "the right thing to do."

Other fellow service members have not been so lucky—witch hunts, jaded lovers, and spiteful peers have outed more than fourteen thousand gay service members. Who can even begin to estimate the amount of expertise and talent we lost to that discriminatory legislation? How could military leaders have allowed a law that forces dishonesty and erodes core values such as integrity and courage to exist for as long as it did? One thing is for certain: my supervisor took a stand that day, in defiance of the official "military answer."

Steven Collins is a second lieutenant in the U.S.
Marine Corps. He has served nine years in aviation
mechanics and has deployed to Iraq twice.*

By the time I was twenty-four, I was out to my parents and to a close female friend. It started to weigh on me that I had never felt accepted by anyone whose opinion I felt could validate me. My parents had to love me; women are less likely to be disgusted by gays. Cherry-picked anecdotes about acceptance could be found on television or in print, but I had never heard a male friend that I admired speak well of a gay person.

At that point, my closest friend was also a professional peer who I had worked with for over a year. Adam* and I had a great deal of respect for and trust in each other. He had a strong reputation among our group of soon-to-be Marine officers: he was a talented athlete, he had a reserved demeanor, and his character was admirable. After painstaking contemplation, I decided he was ideally suited to pass judgment on my worth as a Marine—and, on some level, as a fellow human being. I reckoned that if Adam, who knew more about me personally and professionally than almost anyone in my life, did not accept me as a friend, or a Marine, because I was gay, then I had been right to be ashamed. He could only come to that decision, I thought, if there was in fact something fundamentally vile or subhuman about me.

Deciding how to come out to Adam was extremely difficult. I felt myself becoming distant from my friends and very distracted from my responsibilities. I was terrified of what he might say when I confessed I was a homosexual. Looking back, I wonder if the reason I went through with it was because he'd noticed a change in my behavior. He approached me and asked if I was all right. I told him I was not, which led him to push further. That made me feel safe enough to say I needed to speak to him in private about a serious issue in a few days.

Several days later I found myself sitting across from Adam at my dining room table. We had driven to my home in near silence. At this point in my life I had lived through my fair share of adversity, but sitting at my table that night brought more shame and fear than I had ever known. For the first time in memory, I could not bring myself to make eye contact with a man. I felt like a criminal. Staring at the pattern of the wooden table, I asked Adam to sit, listen, and judge without interrupting me, noting also that I'd likely be rambling as I struggled to put a painful revelation into words.

It took more discipline than I thought I possessed to keep my voice steady and free of cracks during my rambling confession, and now I felt myself coming apart inside. I looked up and saw that his expression read as though he was concerned. He seemed free of any hatred or disgust, and without any feeling of betrayal. I needed a beer. Still afraid to prompt him for a response, I decided that whether or not Adam was willing to have a drink with me would be a definitive answer in itself. If I remember correctly, he asked for a Bud Light.

He looked at me for a second as if he didn't know what to say. He accepted the beer, then said, "I'm not gay, but I'm flattered you think highly enough of me to tell me that. It must have been really hard for you, especially being enlisted. Obviously I'm still your friend." Then we got into questions, jokes, explanations, and such. He slept on my couch and I took him home in the morning.

We'd talked for a long time, and although I was not proud of dragging my friend into my pitifully desperate grab at acceptance, I felt an incredible sense of relief. It was almost surreal to think of myself as something better than an obscene lie. I felt whole.

And on a practical level, coming out to Adam even saved me from a humiliating situation following the Marine Corps birthday celebration just two days later. A common friend of ours, after many drinks, decided that my perceived inability to ever date or talk to women at bars justified his direct intervention. He co-opted every member of our party that night and insisted he would not back down until I went to talk to the blond he'd picked out for me—and to do anything else was a disservice to the dress blues I was wearing. I tried every trick and gimmick I had learned over the years to weasel my way out of that kind of situation, but he was having none of it. As more and more of our friends started calling me out, I felt myself reaching a point that felt something like panic. But just before I got there, Adam intervened, saying I obviously had different tastes. He then took my matchmaker friend by the shoulder and went to go talk to the blond woman himself. It's difficult to describe how happy I felt to have made a friend like that. Less than a week prior, I'd doubted that such a thing was even possible.

As I look forward, my greatest hope is that no Marine sees his service, his life, or his career through a lens of shame and self-hate. I am convinced this day is not far off.

Bobat Carpenter* is a sergeant in the U.S. Army currently stationed in South Korea. He has deployed twice to Iraq and once to Afghanistan.

D on't Ask, Don't Tell" meant nothing to me until I met Rick*. I was on my second tour to Iraq in support of Operation Iraqi Freedom and only halfway into my yearlong tour. We met over coffee one day and immediately clicked. We connected on a level I had never experienced before. However, I stayed grounded. Regardless of where my thoughts and feelings were taking me, Rick and I were never to be. He was redeploying home in a week, and I wasn't due back for another six months. We were stationed at the same base in Fort Campbell, Kentucky, but I didn't keep any hopes up of seeing him again. The military has a way of keeping people apart—gay or straight.

We hung out as much as possible over his last week in Iraq. Whatever down time I could get I spent with Rick. Saying good-bye to him was bittersweet. While it's always nice to see fellow soldiers head home safely, I wanted my friend with me.

When Rick messaged me for the first time from the States, I was so excited. I was officially smitten for the first time in my life. We continued to chat online as much as possible and kept in touch for the remainder of my deployment. We talked about everything—everything, that is, except dating, relationships, love. It felt too taboo.

I made it home safely from that deployment, and all I could think about was seeing Rick again. I was home a month before my birthday. All I wanted for my birthday was to go on a date with Rick. It would be my first date as a gay man. It wouldn't matter where we went, what we did, or how romantic it was. I just wanted to see what a real date felt like. I expressed my birthday wish to Rick over the phone, and asked him to think about it.

I celebrated my birthday that year without Rick. I didn't hear from him for two months. Field exercise? Temporary duty assignment? Deployed again? After all, he was in a security forces unit. The first month I tried to convince myself the Army and its training were to blame. The second month I convinced myself I'd done something wrong.

Those two months passed and Rick finally called again. We decided to meet at my apartment to discuss everything. I was so angry with him. When I opened the door, I was ready to tell him off. Then he smiled. I forgot everything.

We talked about all that had happened. I told him of my anger; he told me of his fear.

"Two guys can't date in the Army," he said. "It is wrong." He continued on about the rules, about DADT, about discharge. "Even if nobody found out about us, married soldiers with families make it farther in the Army than single soldiers. We can't risk our careers over dating."

I had a short response: "I love you."

I won't lie and say I fought back tears. There weren't any to hold back. He'd used a word that both of us had a conditioned response to: "soldiers." We were *soldiers*. Above all else, we were soldiers.

It was scary enough to tell him I loved him. It was even scarier when I asked if he loved me in return. "You know the answer to that," he replied. Our meeting ended with a hug and a kiss on the forehead. No more words were necessary. Our friendship—our relationship?—ended as abruptly as it had begun.

The next time I saw Rick was at church four months later; it was just four days short of a year since we'd met. He was sitting with a woman who I presumed was his wife. I offered no emotion on my face when we made eye contact, nor did he. Did it hurt? Absolutely. But we were soldiers—we still *are* soldiers.

We had both expected a rough life under "Don't Ask, Don't Tell." We didn't expect to fall in love.

Rick, I know where you are. You know where I am. We haven't spoken in years, but I know we still think about each other when our heart aches for its other half. I miss you. I love you.

*Jameson Lamie is a first lieutenant in the
U.S. Air Force. He is currently a force support
officer at Andrews Air Force Base, Maryland.*

Like a lot of straight guys, I never knew what to think about homosexuals. My small-town upbringing was immediately followed by four years at the Air Force Academy, which meant that my only exposure to gay men and women were the caricatures I saw in the media. This portrayal of homosexuality was too different and dramatic for me to completely understand. I was a twenty-three-year-old guy seemingly supportive of equality yet uncomfortable with the idea of homosexuality.

"Don't Ask, Don't Tell" had been intended to protect homosexuals in the military, but in reality it left them defenseless and fostered discrimination within the military. Locker room talk flourished in the open-bay showers at the Academy, and the homophobic jokes were never ending. I must confess that I shared in a laugh or two about gay flamboyance or exuberance. Why do they talk like that? Why do they dress like that? I didn't believe I could ever consider a homosexual a *real* friend, a friend I could treat like one of the guys.

I'll never forget the night that my perspective completely changed. I'd spent over two months with a group of guys during an Air Force training course, and we were carpooling to Alabama for another professional development program in January 2010. We stopped along the way in Charlotte for a night on the town. As we started to explore what the city had to offer, my friend Josh pulled me aside and told me he was gay. I really didn't know what to think; it was completely unexpected. He was such a typical guy's guy. He was more into sports than theater. He wore jeans and T-shirts rather than pastels and hair gel. He ordered beer at the bar rather than cosmopolitans. "I support you," I told him, and I assured him that his secret was safe with me. The surprising thing was that I meant it. I knew a few people at civilian universities who were gay, and I had wrestled around in my mind about what I would say if one of my friends in the military came out to me. As open-minded and tolerant as I seemingly was, I thought I would have to tell a white lie by giving my support. But when I was blindsided by Josh, that all changed. When I gave him my support, I meant it. The rest of the night in Charlotte unfolded much as the previous nights together as a group, and we carried on without any mention of Josh's secret.

Over the next six weeks of the program, Josh and I talked about a lot of things. I was still baffled by how my friend could be gay. I felt I was tolerant of homosexuality, but the homosexual lifestyle I saw on TV was disturbing and bizarre. Before, I thought people had the right to engage in homosexual behavior, but I questioned the authenticity of their feelings for one other. I felt it was their craving for legitimacy in society that caused them to declare their love for one another, and I didn't think their love could ever match the love that a man and woman feel toward each other.

I'd had all those misconceptions until I met Josh. After a few weeks, Josh recognized my genuine interest in him as a friend and started opening up to me a bit more. He mentioned that he had journal entries from his time at the Academy about dealing with his sexuality, and he shared a few of them with me. He wrote at length of the heartfelt emotions he felt toward another man, but how the guy had sadly slipped away. It wasn't just words on paper; I could tell he'd captured real, genuine, passionate feelings in his journal. It was surprising because he'd described the same emotions that overcame me when I met my now fiancée. Of course, *I* was able to stop everyone in my squadron and tell them about how head over heels in love I was . . . but not Josh. My fiancée means everything to me, and she is an integral part of my understanding who I am as a person. I cannot fathom keeping my emotions toward her hidden from my family and friends.

Following our six weeks together, the four of us went to our separate bases across the United States. I continue to stay in close contact with Josh, who recently came out to his conservative family. While I was nervous they would shun him, they welcomed Josh with open arms and have been supportive of this previously hidden side of his life. Being gay in America is difficult in itself, but I have seen a glimpse of how being gay in the military is even more arduous than the average American can imagine. I don't know how Josh kept everything to himself. I applaud his bravery, as putting on a facade was an important part of his everyday routine.

Having met Josh, I firmly believe that ignorance is the biggest opponent to the acceptance of homosexuality. We fear what we do not understand, and forcing people to stay in the closet only perpetuates this ignorance. The repeal of "Don't Ask, Don't Tell" only opens the door for tolerance and understanding; individual military members are the ones who will need to step through that door. I hope there are more Joshes in our military who can share their stories and promote understanding of what it means to be gay. It certainly won't happen overnight, but I am a prime example of how minds can be changed one at a time.

*Justin Crockett Elzie is a former U.S. Marine
Corps sergeant. Wanting to make a difference,
he came out publicly on* **ABC World News** *in
January 1993. He became the first Marine
discharged under "Don't Ask, Don't Tell,"
but was later reinstated, becoming the first Marine
to challenge the policy with a federal lawsuit.
He went on to serve four years while openly gay.*

W hen President Clinton announced the "Don't Ask, Don't
Tell" policy he called it "a major step forward." Nothing
could have been further from the truth. I had come out earlier that
year on national television to try to make a difference, and was
serving as an openly gay Marine. The Marines had already moved
to try to discharge me, and once the president announced the policy I knew it would just be a matter of time before they issued the
order to kick me out. Sure enough, on August 27, 1993, I was called
up to the battalion headquarters at Camp Lejeune, North Carolina,
to see the personnel officer. When I arrived, I reported to her and

asked her what was going on. She told me that I was to be discharged by Wednesday, September 1. This gave me only four working days to check out. She instructed me to start the process of turning in my military gear and checking out of my unit ASAP.

With a pretentious attitude, she handed me my checkout sheet and said, "Hurry up and check out." She couldn't wait to see me gone at that point, as she didn't think gays should be in the Marines. I walked out of her office and got a copy of the dismissal notice from Marine headquarters. As I read the message, I noticed that a document review stamp was on it and several officers in the battalion had already read and signed it. The battalion legal officer had signed it and put a smiley face next to his signature. They were all so glad that I was finally going to be gone. They would no longer have to deal with having an openly gay Marine serving in their unit.

I walked around in shock as I prepared to check out. I had been a Marine for ten years. It was hard to believe I was being kicked out. What was I going to do now? I couldn't sleep and I was having stress headaches as the day of reckoning neared.

September 1, the day of dismissal, came fast. When I saw the warrant officer at check-in, she told me with a sneering attitude that it didn't matter if I hadn't finished by the end of the day. "You're going to be gone today," she said, and then curtly turned around and walked off.

As I sat down at the administrative clerk's desk to finish up some paperwork, he asked me for my military ID card. I froze as I realized what was happening. I reached for my wallet and opened it, then pulled out my ID card and handed it to him. I suddenly felt like I was losing a part of myself, a part of my identity. He took my ID card, opened the drawer of his desk, and pulled out a huge pair of scissors. As I watched in horror, the clerk cut up my ID card right in front of me. At that moment I wanted so much to order him to stop, but I couldn't. My eyes filled with tears and a lump swelled up in my throat as I saw ten wonderful years pass right before my eyes and I realized a part of me was now gone. Everything I had known and loved about the Marine Corps for the last ten years was being taken away from me. I was an exemplary Marine, but because I had said I was gay, my performance didn't matter.

Over the next two months, my civilian attorneys got a judge to issue an injunction. I was reinstated in the Marine Corps and went on to serve four more years openly gay. Over the course of those four years, I came to realize that I had outgrown the Marine Corps. On February 18, 1997, I was discharged and walked away from the Marines with my dignity and my self-worth. I had made the grade and earned the title of U.S. Marine and at the end of the day nobody could take that away from me.

Daniel W. Hill is a petty officer third class and chaplain's assistant in the U.S. Navy currently stationed at Camp H. M. Smith in Hawaii. He intends to pursue master's degrees in law and financial management in London once he's completed his active service.

The United States Navy had prepared me for many things I would encounter while deployed with the Marines to Afghanistan. There was weapons training, security briefings, culture classes, and even training to recognize and deal with combat-related stress. One thing neither branch prepared me for was what to do when your chain of command begins to discriminate against you, mistreat you, and haze you because of your sexual orientation.

When I arrived in Afghanistan, the initial shock hit me hard: there was a war going on and I was now a part of it. My job as a chaplain's assistant is fairly simple, and can be broken down into three basic tasks: protect the chaplain, set up for various religious services, and provide administrative assistance. According to the Geneva Conventions, chaplains are not allowed to carry or operate a weapon, which makes my job of protection particularly important.

Unfortunately, the chaplain I was assigned to protect in Afghanistan had an ugly attitude, a sharp tongue, and a rather foul mouth. I did my best to ignore his comments. When he began to question my sexual orientation with others within my chain of command, however, I could no longer ignore him. I began to document the statements I'd overheard, or that friends had witnessed. I needed to prepare myself for the worst. My mother herself had suffered discrimination within her unit in the Army, and I knew from her example how to handle this situation with grace and professionalism.

I began to seek the counsel of several senior enlisted leaders and officers outside of my chain of command as well as legal professionals within our command. This led to the decision to formally file an equal opportunity and harassment complaint. When I sat before my commanding officer and explained the situation, she was appalled that something like this was occurring in her unit. She explained, however, that there was nothing she could do to the chaplain legally, as the military did not recognize sexual orientation as an equal opportunity issue. This caused me great dismay. I felt it was hard enough to be an African American in the United

States, with its still fresh wounds from racism, and now I had to deal with the onslaught of gay hatred and bias as well. I felt betrayed by my own country and comrades.

I decided to drop my complaint, but my work was far from over. I was reminded of the many soldiers, sailors, airmen, and Marines serving who might be dealing with a similar situation. It immediately gave me a sense of purpose. I had to go through this experience in order to educate others. Although my fairy godmother never showed up to whisk me away from this awful situation, God and Lady Liberty taught me valuable lessons nonetheless. They would deny me my basic liberties because they knew that would motivate me to work to ensure the liberties of others. I intend to continue to write about this, and speak out and encourage others to speak out against discrimination in any form. Because if we cannot be united ourselves as a country, how do we intend to set an example for the world? The final repeal of "Don't Ask, Don't Tell" is the first step toward ensuring there is indeed, as our founding fathers intended, life, liberty, and the pursuit of happiness for all.

Jamar Green is a lieutenant in the U.S. Navy.
He currently teaches naval tactics at the
Royal Saudi Naval Forces School.

It was an unremarkable mid-April day like so many others. Sitting at my desk, I unbuttoned the top of my drill uniform to allow the cool Annapolis breeze to soothe my sweat-drenched body. At the Naval Academy we practiced marching once, sometimes twice a week during parade season. Every Friday following the parade, Billy* would come to my room for some much needed escape. We were best friends. We discussed family, relationships, our difficult classes, the latest gossip, even the parades that we dreaded so much. This unremarkable Friday, however, Billy never showed. I called his roommate, but he could not account for Billy after their second-period class. Something felt gravely wrong.

My worst fear darted to the front of my mind: *Someone found the note!*

I knew he didn't want to write it, but I'd persuaded him to let his crush know how he felt. What was the worst that could happen?

We saw him every day behind the register at the Mid Store. Billy thought he was cute, and I only wanted my friend to find the happiness he longed for. In the letter we drafted together, he not only explained how he felt but also apologized if his attraction seemed offensive. We didn't know if the object of Billy's affection was gay. Billy delivered the note the very day I suggested he write one. I'd considered the whole thing harmless, although a dark worry began to loom over my subconscious after the note was delivered. I ignored it and thought nothing more of the matter.

The Monday following the parade, I learned that Billy had become the focus of an Article 32 investigation into his alleged homosexuality. While I was waiting for Billy after the parade, he was being questioned. His entire future was up in the air.

As soon as I learned what had happened to Billy, a deep, stalking fear consumed me: *Am I next?* Had I known a few personal words on such a small piece of paper could generate such lifealtering consequences, I never would have suggested he write that note. While it was fear that I felt first, anger followed. I realized that despite my love for America and my willingness to die for her, she did not recognize or protect my sovereignty as she did her heterosexual sons and daughters. DADT forced me to deny who I was; it forbade me to exist while craftily denying me any sliver of defense against antigay harassment. At that moment, I vowed to continue my military career despite the professional and personal sacrifices that I knew I would have to make in the future in order to live a lie.

Both Billy and I finished college, but he transferred to a different school at the conclusion of the investigation. I retained my commission and currently serve as a lieutenant in Saudi Arabia. "Don't Ask, Don't Tell" took what had simply been a youthful crush and turned it into a legal process that ended my best friend's education at the Naval Academy and left me with a great disdain for the United States Navy.

Robert Mobley is a first lieutenant in the U.S. Air Force. He is currently stationed at Gunter Annex, Maxwell Air Force Base, Alabama.

I really did not come to terms with my true identity until about partway through the United States Air Force Academy. I always thought I was gay, but I did not want to admit it to myself. Then, finally, I'd had enough. I admitted it to myself and then to my best friend. But then I left to spend my spring semester as an exchange student at the United States Coast Guard Academy. I was back in the closet again. I didn't know any of the other four Air Force Academy cadets that went there with me, and I felt alone. That changed pretty quickly, though—since there were only five of us in a new place, we all bonded. Not to mention the Coast Guard Academy is the size of a typical high school; everyone knows everyone.

I became close with one Air Force Academy cadet in particular. Ben* and I had the same interests; we would run and work out together, visit Boston and New York together. That spring we decided to go on our spring break together, so we went ahead and booked our trip on a cruise that left out of New York. The plan was to travel to New York on a Friday, spend the night, and sail out the next day. As soon as Friday classes were over, Ben and I hiked down to the train station and headed off to the city. We arrived at about six o'clock in the evening. We went to an expensive steak restaurant, and someone ended up paying our tab when they found out we were military. After dinner the night was still young. We couldn't just go back to the hotel room and sleep; we had to have a night out on the town.

Little did I know that these next few moments would change the rest of my life. Ben asked what sort of club I'd like to go to. A good dance club, I said. We started walking uptown and passed a few. I really did not want to go to a straight club—I'd had enough of living a lie. As we walked, we passed by a very popular gay club. You could tell everyone inside was having a great time. Ben jokingly said, "How about we head in there?" I must have somehow indicated my enthusiasm, because Ben's facial expression changed instantly. "You know that's a gay club, right?" Ben asked. "Yes, I know," I said, "but it looks fun." Ben replied, "Let's go inside and check it out." I was shocked. We walked in and ordered a few drinks. Then Ben said, "You really don't have to explain anything to me if you don't want to. Let's just have a good night." So we did. We danced and danced and danced. I probably had the best time out that I had ever had before in my life.

When we got back to the hotel room, I told Ben I was gay. I told him I just couldn't live a lie anymore and I had to tell him. I also explained that I understood if he didn't want to go on the cruise with me anymore. "Are you crazy?" he said. "Hell, tonight was the most fun I've had in forever. I knew you were gay; I just wanted you to tell me in your own time. By the way, I don't have a problem with it. Just don't get me too drunk." I smiled and went to sleep.

To this day, Ben is still my best friend and he is the very reason I stopped living a lie.

*Tim Walker is a lieutenant colonel and career officer
in the U.S. Air Force with over twenty-three years of
active duty. He has deployed multiple times and is
currently a pilot in the Air National Guard.*

In 1986, after graduating from high school, I enlisted in the United States Air Force. Upon completion of basic military training and technical training, I was assigned to Kirtland Air Force Base in New Mexico. There, I attended the noncommissioned officer's preparatory course, finishing as a distinguished graduate, and later attended Airman Leadership School, where I received the Commandant's Leadership Award.

During my career, I deployed in support of humanitarian and military operations in Panama, the Persian Gulf, Turkey, Somalia, Afghanistan, and Iraq. I was on assignment in Germany in 1993 when "Don't Ask, Don't Tell" was implemented.

It wasn't until after September 11, 2001, when I was deployed to Afghanistan and Iraq and realized there was a very real possibility I could die, that "Don't Ask, Don't Tell" truly became a reality to me. I could not list my partner as a dependent on any forms. What were my rights—what were his rights—if I was hurt or incapacitated or killed? He would not even get notification if the worst happened. He was not eligible for my pension, benefits, visitation rights, counseling, or even the flag from my coffin if I died.

Most people in my unit now know about my sexuality and that I have had a partner for more than four years. A lot of them want to meet him. I realize, though, that one little slipup in front of the wrong person could take the command of my unit away from me, destroy my life as I know it, and ruin everything I have worked for.

My friends who know, tell me that not only am I in the closet, but I am living proof that the whole Air Force is a big closet. They think I'm crazy for remaining in the military, yet here I am still doing my job to the best of my ability and proudly serving my country every day. To this day, when I put on my uniform and look in the mirror, I get misty eyed thinking of all the men and women who have gone before me and worn this uniform.

Having served for over twenty years now and lived with "Don't Ask, Don't Tell" for nearly all of it, I wonder daily what I am still doing here. Why do this to myself and my caring partner? This isn't about me; it's about serving the country I love even though some days I have doubts that it loves me back. It's about being better than the country I love. It's about doing the right thing.

Jack Stevens* is a captain in the U.S. Army working in military intelligence. He has over nine years of service and is currently stationed in the Washington, D.C., area.

I was commissioned through Reserve Officer Training Course as a second lieutenant on active duty in August 2002. When I was commissioned, I knew I was gay. I'd known since about my sophomore year in college when I took my scholarship. I had come out in college to my parents and brother, who was already an officer on active duty, and felt fortunate that they had accepted it without issue.

I kept things rather quiet about my sexuality from 2002 until September of 2005, when I came out to the first person I felt I could trust in my unit. On my birthday weekend in September of 2005, I had spent time with my boyfriend in a hotel so we could be together. I lied and told friends I was visiting my cousin. When I got back, my close friend Steve* asked me how the weekend was. I knew Steve was someone I could trust, so I decided to tell him the truth. Much to my surprise, he simply smiled, said, "That's cool, deuce," gave me a hug, and pulled my birthday cake out of the oven. It was definitely a positive first experience and something that made my life easier as we went to Iraq in November. Steve was there for me to talk to when I couldn't talk to anyone else about how my relationship was going and needed to vent. Somewhere around June of 2006, Steve and I were sitting around with two of our fellow captains, Mark* and Tim*, chatting after we'd smoked cigars and drank some beer. At the end of the night, I told them I was gay. Mark and Tim were floored. The first thing out of Mark's mouth was, "Dude, I'm sorry for all the gay jokes." I just about fell on the floor when he said that, because I'd never taken offense to anything since it was always in good fun. Tim took it a bit harder: the news took the breath out of him so fast you would have thought I'd kicked him in the stomach, the way he was coughing. He was a little distant for about a week and a few days, but never said he had a problem with it.

After coming out to them, I became more comfortable sharing information. About a month later another friend in my unit stopped by my room to borrow some movies and noticed pictures on my computer. He inquired who the guy was and I told him it was my boyfriend. He wanted to know the details about him, how long we'd been together, etc. It was a nice response to get. Soon after, I told my friends from college, who were also all in the military. They were very accepting and their only concern was why I hadn't told them sooner.

When I returned from deployment, I began coming out to more people. The conversations weren't always easy. One colleague simply stopped hanging out with me and stopped talking to me. That went on for a good two years until I'd come back from my second deployment and he was finishing up his second deployment with a different unit. He e-mailed me out of the blue one day apologizing for his reaction and his actions. He then proceeded to invite me to his wedding, which I ended up being a part of. To this day we hang out regularly and we have restored our previous friendship. I forgave him without a second thought because we had been through a great deal together during deployment and it took a great deal of maturity and pride swallowing on his part to contact me and apologize.

I have been very fortunate in my journey of coming out to people under DADT and know that not everyone has had the same fortune I have. I am thankful for my friends for accepting me and making me realize that my sexuality wasn't something I needed to hide. I continue to be selective of who I tell, not because I am afraid of who I am but because I know not everyone is so accepting and therefore not everyone needs to know. People know who I am based on my work and how I treat my soldiers, not because of rumors about who I sleep with. My personal life will continue to be just that, and I will continue to let those people in whom I can trust and who have earned my respect enough to truly get to know me.

Jonathan Cagle was a combat medic in the
Illinois Army National Guard.
He currently resides in Phoenix, Arizona.

I finished my service contract with the Army National Guard in October of last year, upon completion of my stop-loss tour in Afghanistan. I received positive feedback from leadership, and was often reassured that I was one of the best medics in my battalion. I spent most of my tour in remote outposts, often as the only medical asset available to our small teams. The year following a combat tour is obviously tumultuous, and every day I experience that unreal moment when I want nothing more than to be back on the Pakistan border, convoying all over the Hindu Kush mountains.

Then I remember the additional burden of stress that DADT caused me during my deployment. Being a combat medic for an infantry battalion made it impossible for me to confide my sexual identity to any of my peer soldiers. I was stationed at a combat outpost in an isolated part of the country with a team of nine people. Those bonds transcend almost any relationship I've known—I will never share so close and intense an experience with anyone else in my life. I know I could call any of these men and they would be there to help me no matter what the consequences. None of these people are aware that I am gay, which means an incredibly important piece of my personal life is hidden from those closest to me. My strongest friendships are based on nontruths.

It was also incredibly difficult for my home life. Before I left for Afghanistan, I had to sit down with my mother and boyfriend to develop an alert plan in case anything happened to me during the deployment, because my boyfriend would obviously not be notified. The few times we spoke on the phone, I had to use feminine pronouns with him. We didn't really have an actual conversation throughout the course of my deployment, because there isn't a private room for telephone use. It's a common space, and there are always people around. I hated the idea of lying about my relationship, so I generally acted as though I didn't have one. After playing that role for a year, it started to become true in my head.

Along with my relationship suffering, I lost a part of my identity. Faking straight for 365-plus consecutive days eventually reformats your identity. I'm not as comfortable being me anymore.

The pain of serving under DADT was perhaps clearest when I returned home from deployment. There's this amazing moment when you get home: you roll into a high school gym (or some place like it) plastered in red, white, and blue. Your entire family is there waiting, bursting with joy to get to you. They release you from your formation and there's a mad dash. All those wives and girlfriends sprint into the formation to finally wrap their arms around their men. It seems corny, but it's almost like a small consolation for the personal hell each of these relationships has experienced. When I came home, I asked my boyfriend not to come. I didn't want to risk it. But my mom and dad—a retired master sergeant—insisted that he be there. When I broke free from the formation, my boyfriend just had to stand there, a family friend, and politely shake my hand. I asked him not to cry at the ceremony because it could be a give-away. I can't imagine how hard that was for him.

Master Sergeant Alexander has been in the
U.S. Marine Corps for over seventeen years.*

When I was a second-cycle drill instructor at Edson Range in 2004, I had the unfortunate experience of witnessing a recruit emotionally break after disclosing to his chain of command that he was gay. His name was Recruit Jordan*. I don't know if he came forward as a means to get out of the Marine Corps or if he felt morally compelled to tell his senior drill instructor (DI) about his sexual orientation. Apparently he had received a letter from his boyfriend, who could not accept the fact that he was joining the Marines—he didn't want him to go to Iraq and get killed. This was the year when the Fallujah battle was at its peak. Unfortunately, his boyfriend broke up with him and Jordan became depressed.

But Recruit Jordan didn't break because he was heartbroken. He broke because, after he came out, he was brutally mocked by the DIs and recruits in his company. Once the news was let out, it was a constant gauntlet of gay jokes and remarks from the DIs. It made my stomach turn. There wasn't a thing I could do about it due to fear that I might get exposed myself and be released for being gay. I wish I could have done something about it. But I didn't.

All recruits slept in bunked racks and Jordan had a top rack. So one night, Recruit Jordan tied a tent rope around his neck to a pack and pushed it off his rack. He wanted to kill himself. His rack mate below stopped him and the fire watch woke up the duty drill instructor in the process. Jordan was immediately pulled from his platoon. He had a nervous breakdown, and was seen by a psychologist in medical. Later he was processed for separation for attempted suicide and released, but nothing was done to the drill instructors that had provoked this mess. I believe the drill instructors that harassed Jordan did so to break him down and push him out of the military. They wanted him out of there, and it is easier to discharge a recruit with suicidal ideations than to dismiss under DADT.

I tell this story to fellow service members because I want them to know firsthand what damage can be done when you disclose your sexual orientation to your command. Many gay service members go to great lengths to hide their secret lives. I know I did.

During my time at the recruit depot, I went from senior drill instructor to chief drill instructor. I was able to persuade recruits not to out themselves to the company staff. I was able to inspire them to stay in and finish their enlistment without fear of exposure. I was careful how I worded my counseling sessions, but I got my message across: *Stay in. If I can do seventeen years, so can you.*

I push people to stay in because I don't want them to end up like Recruit Jordan. The double life that so many of us have to endure takes its toll, but it's a necessity if you want to survive in the military.

Recruit Jordan, if you happen to read this story, I am so sorry I couldn't help you on that cold, gloomy day when the drill instructors antagonized you. I am sorry I was not strong enough to stop it. I hope you're living a happy, fruitful life, and I pray that God is taking care of you.

Jacob Smith* is a pilot in the U.S. Navy and
is currently stationed in the United States.

I was getting ready for the packers to show up to move my household goods from my apartment off base when my phone rang.
It was my leading petty officer (LPO), Bill*. I was off from work that
day, so I thought it was a little unusual he would call, but not out of
the realm of normal. Still, I had the usual twinge of fear I got anytime someone from work called me at home. Was today the day I
was going to be investigated? No matter how many times I got a call
from work, the thought always crossed my mind, even three years
into my enlistment.

"Hey, what's up, man? Did you know the command master
chief tried to get you kicked out for being gay?" Bill was an excel-
lent LPO, and he never minced his words. It was every nightmare
from the last three years of my life come true in a few short seconds on the phone. My heart dropped, I started sweating, I stam-
mered on the phone. "Uh, no, what the hell?" I asked, trying to
sound like the thought was absurd to me. "Yeah," he replied. "Did

you leave a computer online at work and have someone log you on to Gay.com as a joke or something?"

No, I thought to myself, *I logged on myself.* I would never admit that to him, because I was still petrified of the Navy Criminal Investigation Service knocking on my door. The truth is, I logged on to Gay.com from the barracks every night to talk to the only three or four other gay men I knew in the military; it was my very small but important support network. It took me over a year in the service to meet only a handful of my fellow gay service members.

I tried my best to calmly play off the questions on the phone and to get as much information from my LPO as I could, but I couldn't shake the feeling that my entire world was about to come crashing down at the worst possible time. I called my boyfriend, crying and panicked, as soon as Bill hung up the phone.

You see, the move I was getting ready for was no normal permanent change of station, but my orders to go to the Naval Science Institute and start the Navy's coveted Seaman to Admiral–21 commissioning program. It was the most highly touted and competitive commissioning program for enlisted sailors, and it was a tremendous opportunity. The Navy was about to pay me active duty pay while I attended college full-time at the university of my choosing, and it was going to pick up the tuition as well. After graduation, the Navy would send me to flight school.

It was all a dream come true. My family was incredibly proud of me, my friends excited for me, all my coworkers congratulatory and wishing me the best as I was about to check out of the command. And with one phone call from my LPO, I thought I'd lost all of it. I felt like every single thing I had worked for in the last three years of my life was about to be taken away from me because I was gay.

I could not sleep for two days. I was inconsolable. I walked on eggshells at work, questioning every glance from my chief or my division officer. After two days, the realization hit me like a ton of bricks. The investigation Bill had told me about had happened two years prior. Since then I had had two wonderfully long years of good evaluations, effusive praise from my supervisors, awards for being junior sailor of the quarter, letters of recommendation from my entire chain of command for a commissioning program, personal mentorship from my command master chief and my executive officer. All these people in my chain of command had known about me for two years and it hadn't mattered to them. The only thing they cared about was how hard I worked.

This realization was the most liberating feeling you could imagine. My life of paranoia and fear was a self-imposed prison serving no purpose other than to try to continue in compliance with "Don't Ask, Don't Tell." Being gay in the military doesn't interfere with unit cohesion; "Don't Ask, Don't Tell" does. I made myself an outsider from some of the best people I've ever met for no damn reason.

I'd love to say that I have since come out to all of my fellow service members. That would be a lie, however. I have served another five years in relative silence since that phone call. It was bittersweet to find out that my command knew about me and didn't care, as I found out only on my way out the door. "Don't Ask, Don't Tell" has still prevented me from trusting my fellow service members completely, even with that experience under my belt. True unit cohesion won't be possible until every service member can serve with full honesty.

Patrick Twomey is a captain and
physician of internal medicine for the U.S. Army.

I first entered the Army as part of the Health Professions Schol-arship Program. I remember reading the documents that said, "I will not partake in homosexual activities," when I was signing up, but as I hadn't come out even to myself at that point, it didn't seem to pertain to me. But when I went to medical school in Washington, D.C., that quickly changed. I developed a crush on one of my roommates, and we ended up coming out to each other a few months into the school year.

After that moment, my life changed for the better. I was living in one of the most liberal and progressive cities in the country, made great friends, and studied with well-educated and worldly colleagues who supported me wholeheartedly. It was a dream. I almost completely forgot I was in the Army. My senior year I even met a great guy and started an amazing relationship. I had been promised a spot for residency at Walter Reed.

Then the reality of the Army hit. I was reassigned to Hawaii for residency based on "the needs of the Army." I was devastated! Sure, being stationed in a tropical paradise doesn't give you much room for complaint, but it was six thousand miles away from my support network, friends, family, and boyfriend. All at once I was beginning to understand the reality of the military, and also the particular difficulties of being gay in the military. Straight soldiers can go to their battle buddies, friends, commanders, chaplain, or even physicians to discuss their feelings. But I had no one. I was moving to a new command with new people I didn't know and would be on active duty for the first time. I had no idea how this would play out. All I knew was that I could be kicked out if I told anyone the real reason I was upset.

When I arrived in Hawaii, I met my intern class. They were a very nice bunch from all over the country, but I had no idea how they would respond if I told them I was gay. As a result, I kept to myself a lot. I moved to Waikiki to be closer to gay bars and ended up making some new friends there, but it was still very difficult to maintain my two separate lives in a small city. Slowly, the walls started falling and one by one each of my colleagues found out my secret.

I began by telling people I thought would be open-minded, but a couple months into residency, I decided to tell the first of my straight male friends. His response was one of the funniest reactions I have experienced yet. He grew up in a very conservative household and got married right after college. Even though he went to medical school in Philadelphia, he claimed he had never "knowingly" met a gay man before.

One evening we met in a small bar with another friend, a female friend who already knew my secret. He asked me about a date I had recently been on. The conversation went roughly as follows:

"So what was your date like?"

"Um, pretty good. I had a really good time. We're going to see each other again."

"Yeah? Is she hot?"

"I like to think so."

"How tall is she? How long is her hair?"

"Um, she's about six-one and her hair is short—about my length."

"Huh, wow, she's tall. Big breasts?"

"No. Very flat. Honestly, not much bigger than mine."

"Interesting pick. So you like the tall pixie look. Well, when do we get to meet her?"

"Well, that's the tough part—" I cast a knowing glance with a smirk toward my other friend. "I'm actually breaking a pretty big rule dating this person."

"*Oh my god!* . . . She's married?"

"No, bigger."

"She's an attending at the hospital?"

"No."

"She's enlisted?"

"No—well, yes." The guy was enlisted in the Air Force. "But . . . okay, *two* rules, I guess."

And so it went for about five minutes. I finally said, "Think about it. What's another very big rule that you're not allowed to '*ask*' about and I can't '*tell*'?"

Then a lightbulb went off. "*No!* She's a transsexual?"

"Wrong again. No—it's a dude!"

Utter silence.

He was kind of quiet the rest of the night. I worried that I'd misread him and that he might turn me in. A few days later I spoke to his wife, who shared that in reality he was just in shock. But our friendship remained unchanged. It was a good experience to see that my first coming out to a conservative Army colleague was positive, and was actually a mind-opening event for him.

The rest of my residency in Hawaii turned out to be an amazing experience. I ended up meeting a few other gay residents. One of the attendings in my department came out to me as well. I suddenly had a mentor, and was able to confide things in him and his partner. By the time I graduated, everyone in my residency knew my secret. At the senior dinner, the chief of internal medicine at the hospital actually placed a pink lei around my neck and laughed! It was actually very comforting to learn that there are very supportive and understanding people in the military, and that it truly is about the job and trusting the soldier next to you. When it boils down to it, once people know that there already *are* gay people serving right next to them every day, they are forced to think about their views in real terms. And their attitudes will change.

Jenn Brown* is a midshipman at the U.S. Naval Academy, where she aspires to become a pilot in the Navy.

I don't think there was ever a time in my life when I didn't want to serve my country. My dad served, his dad served, and his dad's dad served. It only felt natural for me to follow in their large footsteps. I knew I wanted to join the military even before I knew I was a lesbian.

I remember the day I was accepted into the United States Naval Academy. My mom was so excited she came to the restaurant where I waited tables and made me open the package in front of her. My dad couldn't have been prouder. When I got home, I looked through the package and pulled out my service papers. I remember the document asking me if I had any mental reservations that would keep me from fulfilling my duties. I put the paper down, and my eyes focused on the two words "mental reservation." The truth was, yes, I did have mental reservations. I knew that if

I signed that paper, I would not only be fulfilling my dream of service, but I would also be signing away my personal life, sentencing it to years of dishonesty, hiding, and shame. I kept looking at the paper. Should I sign? Is this what I really wanted? The answer was a resounding yes. Did I want to hide who I was for the rest of my career, maybe even the rest of my life? That answer was a resounding no.

I remember putting the pen down and going outside to get some fresh air. The stars were out that clear Texas night; my thoughts held anything but clarity. I knew if I signed that paper I would be lying, a violation of the very foundation my future school and service were built upon: honor, courage, and commitment. Those three words even appeared on the front of the Naval Academy folder all my papers had come in. I knew signing would violate the first, and possibly most important, of the three. I went back inside. I picked up my pen and signed the paper. I looked at my signature, just barely dried in black ink. I knew I had just committed myself to a life of service, and that I would be fulfilling my dream. I remember the feeling. It was a great one. I also remember the bad taste in my mouth as I mailed the package back to the admissions office. I knew I would have to hide who I really was for—possibly—the rest of my life. That feeling of shame was new for me. It didn't go away for a very long time.

I still had the bad taste in my mouth when I screamed *"I do!"*

with the rest of my classmates as we took our oath of office from the Superintendent of the United States Naval Academy. I was supposed to be committing myself to a life of service to my country. No one around me could know that I was committing myself to a life of lies as well.

I intend for my resignation to offer a concrete example of the consequences of a failed law and policy."

—Katherine "Katie" Miller,
in her West Point resignation letter

Charles Clymer is currently a West Point cadet in his junior year. He is studying political science.

As a straight American, I have never been the target of the prejudice that homosexuals in our country endure, but I have always been aware of the difficulties of being gay in our culture. Still, it wasn't until I entered the United States Military Academy at West Point that I directly encountered deeply entrenched, rabidly antihomosexual sentiments. Very few soldiers there truly possess a hateful perspective, but the views of a few are enough to influence the groupthink mentality that prevails. The culture of hypermasculinity and the overwhelming presence of conservative Christian values within the ranks also contributes to the hostile environment against gays and lesbians. Of course, this isn't true for all soldiers—many, regardless of their personal beliefs and backgrounds, serve with professionalism and respect.

During my sophomore year at West Point, the "Don't Ask, Don't Tell" repeal debate began to heat up on campus. President Obama had promised to repeal the law during his campaign, and it seemed there was a strong chance that the move to overturn the ban would kick into high gear after the midterm elections. The command team, made up of the Superintendent and Commandant, among others, had consistently impressed upon the Corps of Cadets the need to respect others and emphatically communicated that discrimination on any level would not be tolerated. Their leadership was outstanding, but their influence over the culture of the Corps—just like the influence of any commander over his or her brigade—was often negligible. The pervasive groupthink mentality of young cadets dictated that to stand out for any reason, let alone take an unpopular opinion on a highly controversial issue, invited derision and social isolation. I had never experienced anything quite like it, not even in high school.

This made it all the more remarkable when our fellow student Katie Miller resigned from the Corps in protest over "Don't Ask, Don't Tell," stating that she could not serve with honor if she was forced to constantly live a lie about her sexuality. Her decision sent shock waves through campus. We attended endless briefings, classes, and lectures about the importance of moral courage in the face of great opposition. The community should have honored Katie Miller for her choice. Instead, what resulted was a widespread—and very public—backlash against not only Katie Miller but also those who supported her. The few who spoke admirably of her in class or posted words of support on Facebook were swiftly attacked with ignorant, hateful retorts. I experienced this myself when defending her.

Despite all the harassment that straight supporters like myself encountered, there were some positive outcomes as well. Gay cadets approached me and others in confidence because they finally felt safe being able to privately discuss their problems with accepting fellow cadets. These were young men and women who had made the noble decision to serve their country but were forced to live in an environment in which homophobia is accepted if not encouraged. I can hardly imagine the pain lesbian or gay cadets have to endure during their time here.

Of course, DADT was repealed only a few months later, a tribute to Katie Miller and others like her who had the integrity to act on the "culture of honor" that had been drilled into us since our arrival at the Academy.

Katie Miller's brave act has helped to bring about much needed change, both in helping to break down the barrier for gay men and women in uniform to serve openly and also to finally challenge an Academy culture that prizes blind conformity over respect for difference.

Alex Johnson is a petty officer second class
in the U.S. Navy. He has been deployed twice.*

When I first joined the Navy, I felt prepared to deal with serving under DADT. I felt all that was needed was to keep my private life private—nothing to it. I didn't realize how it would isolate me from my shipmates. The casual conversations about family and significant others became complicated to the point that I felt the only way to avoid a compromising situation was to avoid socializing. While I still tried to be sociable (as is inevitable when you work so closely with people), by necessity I was still always very closed off from my shipmates. The biggest test came with deployment, and there was one case in particular, in 2005 and 2006, that seriously tested me.

Part of my preparations for deployment included establishing guidelines for communicating with my significant other. We had to devise a way to hide the true nature of our relationship. So we created Yahoo e-mail addresses under fake names, and we developed a code to mask sensitive language. While I was deployed, if

I wished to tell him I loved him, I would say, "One four three." We put other similar expressions in code so we could speak "freely" to each other. For the most part we were successful, but one thing I hadn't really accounted for was tone of voice. It nearly became my undoing.

I had the displeasure of serving with perhaps the most racist, bigoted sailor in the Navy, and unfortunately my conversations with my boyfriend caught his ear. I had seen him in the phone tent, as I had seen plenty of other shipmates there, and felt I was properly prepared. I never noticed him listening in on my conversations. I assume it was the tone of my voice that gave me away, as my conversations with my boyfriend did invoke strong feelings in me. I also found out that he had taken it upon himself to read my e-mails from my boyfriend. He decided to confront me about his suspicions and told me he intended to out me to purge the Navy of "filth" like me. In any other situation I would have strongly defended myself and my sexuality, but in this instance the threat of being outed, investigated under DADT, exposed to my family, and possibly discharged from the Navy so frightened me that I proceeded to spew homophobic bile in a vain effort to prove I was one of the guys.

One of the reasons I'd felt I could deal with serving under DADT was simply because I'd already lived under "Don't Ask, Don't Tell" within my own family. I was not out to anyone in my family except my sister and my mother. While my sister was accepting, my mother's reaction tore at my soul. After I accidentally outed myself to her, she expressed a great deal of disgust and disappointment; then she refused to speak to me for six months, and when she did, she told me never to speak of my sexuality to anyone again. I had regretfully and painfully taken that demand to heart and did all I could to hide my sexuality from the rest of my family. A DADT discharge would take the two most important things in my life away from me: my family and my Navy career.

My shipmate wasted no time in making good on his threat. My chief informed me that he had come to him with his allegations. He could see the terror in my face. My chief had informed him that he was not in a position to initiate an investigation, which prompted my shipmate to state he was then going to our commanding officer. My chief attempted to offer me some comfort. He said he suspected I was gay but was unconcerned one way or the other as I did my job well. While I appreciated his support, my situation seemed to have gone from bad to worse, and there was no getting around my panic. The thoughts of what might happen kept me up at night. I could barely eat. I could barely work. All I could seem to do was wait for the imminent call to captain's mast, my discharge, and the subsequent ostracism from my family. I'd reached the point of despair.

Early one morning I got up, dressed, proceeded to the armory, checked out my weapon, and headed to the nearby camp storage garage, as it was generally pretty private. I sat for five, maybe ten minutes with the barrel of my rifle under my chin and my finger on the trigger. I felt I'd have nothing left to live for without my family and my Navy service. Then I thought about my boyfriend, my friends, my distaste for running away from problems, and I laid my weapon down. I decided to confront my situation and deal with whatever might happen.

Nothing did happen. For reasons unknown to me, I never was called to captain's mast. For weeks, though, I lived in fear that today would be the day. It affected me to the point that my communication with my boyfriend dropped significantly. I might have called him once a month over the course of that deployment, which deeply hurt our relationship. After that scare, I went beyond just trying to hide my sexuality and began to pretend that I was straight. It was a betrayal of my most valued principle to be true to myself and proud of who I am. It stayed with me for years afterward, affecting my work and my home life. I allowed that incident to tear me down, to frighten me even, and it took a long time for me to get past that. It took a long time before I was once again the hard-charging sailor I'd been in the past.

Kenneth Sprague is in the U.S. Army.
He has been deployed to Germany,
Bosnia, Korea, Iraq, and Kuwait.

I serve in the U.S. Army and have spent long, long periods of time living in small tents with my brothers in arms, in countries like Germany, Bosnia, Korea, Turkey, Iraq, Kuwait, and places you probably couldn't find on a map. I switched to light infantry after about five years, and this meant even more time in the field in remote areas, sharing close quarters in all aspects of life with my fellow soldiers, 99.5 percent who were male.

During the year I spent in Iraq, contact with my then boyfriend was very limited. While my friends were able to communicate openly via phone, e-mail, and letters, and were able to share their difficulties in military family support groups, I had to pretend that my boyfriend was just a "close friend."

When I was able to speak on the phone with "my friend," I was always hypervigilant about what I said, making sure our feelings for each other never became obvious. Many topics were off-limits:

we couldn't talk about our shared past, the goings-on of mutual friends, or current LGBT equality events or legislation in the news. Our talks were so bland at times, I wondered what the point of all the pain was. But just hearing his voice helped so much. I would reread e-mails several times before sending to make sure that the message didn't appear overly friendly. I would make sure that e-mails I sent to other friends covered similar topics so that our correspondence didn't seem unique. Ridiculous as it sounds, that was the level of my fear.

And I was one of the lucky ones. No one in my unit with the 101st Airborne Division—from my battalion commander to my company commander and platoon leader—was on a witch hunt. I can honestly say they did not care about anything other than the mission and making sure that their soldiers were taken care of. The problem was that correspondence—phone, e-mail, post—was monitored outside their area of control, so I never felt like I could relax my guard. I didn't want to let my team down, leaving them a man short in combat operations because I let something slip.

In my experience, one of the worst aspects of "Don't Ask, Don't Tell" was that some soldiers used the policy to get out of deployments to Iraq and Afghanistan, or tried to get shipped home early because they didn't like what they had signed up for. These cowards helped create an impression that gay soldiers are weak, that they would jump ship when the bullets started flying. This was especially damaging because many people in the Army are from small towns or midsize communities and have never known a gay, lesbian, bisexual, or transgendered person. And this might become their first impression. For that, I am eternally sad.

Still, despite all the difficulty, there were happy moments. My best experience under "Don't Ask, Don't Tell" was upon returning home from Iraq. More than a few of my fellow infantrymen knew I was gay, and no one cared. I did take a bit of ribbing and good-natured joking in private, but, to be honest, crude jokes are common in the ranks. However, I didn't know at the time that my commander knew I was gay. Coming home from deployment can be a horrible time for a gay soldier. While everyone else has friends, family, loved ones there to greet them, your circle of gay or lesbian friends can't really attend, can't run up and hug you and give you a kiss and tell you how much they love you and missed you and are so glad you came home safe. You're so paranoid, you don't even want them there, to make sure nothing slips.

Even with his family present, my commander took the time to tell me, quietly, that he was sorry that my friends couldn't be here to welcome me home, and that he was proud to have served with me. Then he shook my hand, letting me know that he knew, and it didn't matter to him.

Brandon Fleharty* is a captain in the U.S. Navy.

O n September 22, 2004, my boyfriend of two years died after I told his doctors to stop further medical intervention. I was lucky enough to have a medical power of attorney that was accepted by the hospital. It was a long and agonizing two weeks watching his health deteriorate from a vibrant twenty-five-year-old former soldier to a bedridden unconscious man.

What ended tragically had started magically. We'd met two years earlier while stationed in the same area. Soon after meeting, we began planning for a long-term future together. He left the Army to allow me to stay on active duty. Our relationship weathered the storms of my deployment and a move to a city neither of us wanted to be in.

Shortly after the move he became quite sick and within a week was in the hospital. That night in the ER the doctors couldn't pinpoint the problem, but through the night they ran various tests including an HIV test. He looked at me and I immediately knew: he was HIV positive and probably was the day we met. He'd known, but had never told me.

When I visited the next day at lunchtime, he told me the news that I already knew. For the next hour he cried and I was silent. For two years he had lied to me and knowingly put me at risk. But my immediate concern was his recovery. The doctors were blunt; his lungs had been badly damaged by a two-week bout of pneumonia. Had I known about his status, we would have sought specific treatment earlier, but I was clueless about it. That day, a patient advocate had us fill out forms granting me powers of attorney. I know now that he knew his prognosis was grave, but he put on a brave face, and I continued to visit as often as I possibly could without raising suspicion at the office.

His condition rapidly deteriorated. His lungs were badly scarred and not functioning. He was placed on a respirator, and soon the doctors induced a coma. I called his parents, whom I'd never met before, and they arrived the next day. About five days later the doctor pulled me aside and said he would pass within the day. If I desired, I could have him resuscitated, but death was inevitable. On Sunday, September 22, he died before my eyes. I told the nurse not to resuscitate him. He was gone.

I went home to confront my grief, and my anger about the years of lies. Until that point I'd had no time to get tested myself. I dreaded finding out that I was positive. I deliberately chose not to get tested until after the funeral for fear the resentment might convince me to not make the trip.

At work, my boss knew I was struggling. He was not a particularly compassionate man, and was clearly not tolerant of gays in the military. When I put in for last-minute leave, he pressed me for a reason. Had my wife been ill and died of cancer, I would have been given as much leave as necessary and the command would have rallied a support network. I was alone in this. I told him that a friend had died and that I wanted to attend the funeral.

I knew I needed to talk to someone. I was new to the town, and had yet to make any friends. My support network was scattered throughout the world. I fell into a deep depression. I certainly could not go to medical and ask to speak to a therapist. There are lots of support systems for service members who lose a spouse or even a girlfriend or boyfriend. For a gay man in the military who has lost a partner, there is nothing.

I eventually went to a civilian psychologist and paid for it myself. This helped extensively but quickly became cost prohibitive. One huge relief was learning my HIV status. I paid for a test at a civilian clinic; if I was positive, I wanted to tell my chain of command on my terms and not have it reported directly. I was HIV negative.

I was soon reassigned and PCS'd to a different location. While still struggling with my emotions and the loss of my partner, I self-medicated with alcohol. I looked into asking for help through the military, but quickly found out that if I revealed my sexuality, even in a substance abuse treatment setting, I would be discharged. The military, with all its resources and safety nets, could provide me nothing and I was unraveling quickly.

Eventually, faced with inevitable self-destruction, I decided to get help. I braced for discharge after fifteen years of service. I was lucky enough to find help in a way that I could address my problems, but I still wasn't being completely honest. I knew my counselor was able to read between the lines, but I feared revealing too much and usually demurred when pressed for details of my life. Many counselors, chaplains, or doctors would not have shown the same compassion. Still, I feared discharge.

After a long struggle, I emerged on the other side. Addiction will stay with me for the rest of my life, and I have dealt with it primarily through civilian support groups. My depression was long-term but did dissipate with time. I can only assume it would have been resolved more quickly had it been diagnosed and treated by a medical professional who could treat me for longer than four months at a time.

My personal tragedies are not unique. They are life situations that affect everyone in the military. The death of loved ones, and the collateral consequences surrounding it, face nearly every person in uniform, and so the military is hypervigilant about providing assistance. But if you're gay, not only are you on your own, the military's answer is discharge. That was my dilemma. I am fortunate enough to have come out intact and have continued my career in the military. Many gay service members in the same situation have not been so lucky.

James Hunter is hospitalman third class and currently stationed at the Navy Branch Health Clinic in Sasebo, Japan.

After boot camp I studied to become a hospital corpsman. I received orders to Japan, and this was to be my first command. I was ambitious and ready to serve. I reported to Japan right before the branch health clinic's Christmas party. I was welcomed aboard by many personnel, including a woman who really wanted to show me around to make sure I was acquainted.

The next week she talked me into going out with her to a restaurant and walk around the Ginza neighborhood. We had a great time at dinner and talked about everything—our families, where we were from, what are plans were.

Later on that night, as we were walking back to base, I asked her if I could tell her something personal and trust her with confidentiality. She agreed, so I proceeded to tell her that I was gay and had a boyfriend back home. She told me she was cool with it, and shared that she had a gay cousin. From that point on, I thought everything was good. I had a friend I could trust and have fun with. Little did I know how she truly felt.

About a month later, my chief pulled me into the office, along with my department head, and asked if I had ever been read my rights. I smiled, thinking he was joking, and said no. The chief then started spouting out Miranda rights. I just stared at him, realizing he was not joking at all.

The chief then told me that I was under investigation for Articles 92 and 120 of the Uniform Code of Military Justice. My mouth dropped. I had no clue what those articles were or why I was being charged with them. Chief continued: "Have you ever told someone something that you shouldn't have?" I stared back, really thought about it, and said, no, not that I was aware of. My chief wanted to ask me more questions, but before he continued he reminded me that I had an option to remain silent and get legal counsel.

I immediately responded that I would like to use my rights and remain silent. Chief told me I had twenty-four hours to get counsel.

I then went to JAG for legal advice and explained what my command wanted to do. The JAG officer reassured me that it was just an investigation and that nothing would come of this. No charges had been brought up against me; it was just a preliminary investigation.

I reported back to my chief with what I'd found out, and the process went on from there. For weeks afterward, I was stressed and depressed, and my work began to falter. Finally, the news came back: the investigation had been dropped. I was so relieved.

But I had to find out who'd made the report. I knew my chief had just left the paperwork in his drawer, so while on duty one day I found the paperwork and read all the statements. The "friend" that I had trusted, lo and behold, had turned me in. I read the report from my senior enlisted leader, which stated that I had told her I was a homosexual and she felt it was her duty to report me for failing to follow the military code. After reading all the documents, I made copies of them so that if this were ever to arise again, I would have evidence.

I never spoke to that woman again. Going from the top of my command to being investigated for a breach of military code was a disgraceful, horrifying, humiliating experience. I will never forget what my supervisor had said to me one week before the investigation: "I wish we had more sailors in the Navy like you."

I will also never forget the whole ordeal of the investigation. Yet I see that I have become stronger knowing how it feels to have something so personal—and so insignificant to the military—made public in front of your command. And I know I will always stand to my code of ethics—always have the courage to get through any situation, have the commitment to stick with it, and have the honor to live after it.

First Lieutenant Karl Johnson is a C-17 pilot
in the U.S. Air Force. He is stationed at
McGuire Air Force Base, New Jersey.

When I began pilot training, I was still somewhat under the impression that even though I wasn't attracted to girls, I might luck out and find a sweet girl that I was compatible enough with that we could tolerate each other forever after. When I met my future close friend Sam*, I even remember thinking she might be a good "last-ditch effort" at heterosexuality. That thought alone would have set off a million warning bells in the mind of a sane man. But I wouldn't allow myself to recognize these signs, because I thought living as a gay man would compromise my dreams of serving my country. Being the stubborn, type A personality I am, I applied the same thinking to my sexuality that I applied to other difficult situations: I'd work harder and harder until I accomplished my goals. Still, no matter how hard I tried, I couldn't force myself to be attracted to women.

Unsurprisingly, things didn't work out with that last-ditch

effort. In fact, when I finally got up the courage to start putting the moves on Sam, she came out to me and told me she had a girl-friend. I couldn't be more relieved. I could give up the charade, and I gained a great friend. We spent countless nights in each other's dorm rooms talking way past midnight, and quickly we grew in-separable. Suddenly I had someone I could be myself around. She eventually helped me to muster up the courage to drive to the near-est major city (well over an hour away) and go to the gay bars. At the end of a stressful week of flying, studying, and pretending to be straight, it was nice to be able to let my guard down and dance.

My classmates started to take it personally when I would miss their Friday night outings. I didn't go to the city every weekend, but it was enough to make some of them take notice and get upset. It didn't take long before the double life took its toll. My friends would ask if I'd be around to join in their plans, and I found it was easier to dodge the question, then not show up. A rift developed between my classmates and me. I understand why they were of-fended; I never provided a real explanation as to what I was doing or where I was going, even if it was as innocent as having pizza and watching a movie with Sam.

The distance eventually grew. My friends got tired of me bail-ing on their plans, so they stopped inviting me. At first this upset me, but I also knew the distance made my double life easier to pull off. Soon they even stopped asking what I did over the weekends—

even though in reality I was at home alone studying most of the time. The less information I divulged about my relationship with Sam, the more serious they assumed things were between the two of us, and the more they left me alone. Toward the end of the year-long program, I knew I couldn't keep up the lies and evasions. I hated pushing away people who should have been my closest friends and I was tired of hurting them.

As a last hurrah, my flight class had planned a trip to Dallas. It was a long weekend and just a few days before we were to find out the aircraft we were going to be assigned to for the rest of our Air Force careers. I was just weeks away from finishing one of the most stressful years of my life, and I wanted to spend some time having fun with my classmates, like old times. I toyed with the idea of coming out to some of the guys I was closest to and felt I could especially trust.

We wanted to go out with a bang, so we celebrated all weekend. There was a Steak 'n Shake next to our hotel, and in our state of half-drunken stupor one night, a milk shake sounded amazing. My two close friends Don* and Ken* decided to join me. We sat down at a table and put our orders in with a particularly flamboyant waiter I'd made eyes with the minute we walked in. As we waited for our shakes, my friends asked me about what Sam and I were planning on doing after pilot training. Once again I insisted we were just friends.

"That's bullshit and you know it," Ken said. Suddenly my heart skipped a beat. I saw my opportunity to come out to them without the long, awkward buildup. I knew I couldn't live with myself if I didn't take it, so I removed my eyes from his, looked down, and replied: "I know." They were both eager to hear what I finally had to say. I couldn't make eye contact with either of them out of fear and shame. I assured them they wouldn't like the answer, but was still resolved to tell them.

It was no sooner than the words "It's because I'm gay" were on my lips that Ken interrupted me, saying, "If I find out you're a fag, I'm going to beat the living shit out of you right here and now." His words stung and I felt my face go flush. At that very instant our gay waiter dropped off our shakes at our table. I'm pretty sure I was the only one who noticed the appalled expression on his face. Not another word was spoken on the subject for the rest of the night. I stared at my Oreo milk shake and did everything I could to hold back my tears.

To this day, I don't blame Ken for his ignorance. If we were both sober and I had approached the subject with him in a more considered way, I think he would actually have been fine with it. Sadly, the conversation did one thing for me: it affirmed my decision to stay in the closet.

I can't help but feel robbed. I feel I was robbed of twenty-plus of the closest friends I could have ever had. Instead of enjoying what should have been some of the most memorable years of my life, I spent them hiding, lying, and pushing people away. I will never let this happen again. As soon as I am able to come out, I hope my explanation of what I have done will make at least some sense to my buddies from my pilot training days.

Bernard Perry is sergeant first class and observer-controller/trainer in the U.S. Army. He is currently stationed at the Joint Multinational Readiness Center in Hohenfels, Germany.

A lot has changed during my time in the military. When I enlisted in January 1989, the application still asked if you were gay. I checked no. Like many seventeen-year-olds, I had not yet discovered my sexuality, so the answer was in part truthful. But deep down inside I knew that ever since I was a little kid I was attracted to men. Of course, I kept that to myself, because I grew up in a society that said gay was not okay. When I first entered the Army, there were no shows like *Will & Grace, Queer as Folk, Noah's Arc*, or any of the MTV reality series showing gays in a positive light. At that time gay people on the screen were usually portrayed as lonely, hopelessly depressed, or suicidal. Some were even portrayed as the sociopathic sexual deviant, and of course there was the ubiquitous effeminate sissy, who was always the big joke, or otherwise got beat up.

So with all the negative reinforcement we received from media and pop culture, it's hard to imagine why anyone would want to announce to the world that they were gay, let alone join any of the branches of the military. At the time I joined, Vietnam was the last major war our country had fought, and after all the shameful drug abuse and racial problems our military endured following that conflict, our military was still in the process of healing itself. It was the all-volunteer Army. It was the "Be All You Can Be" Army. Joining the Army was seen as the way to make a man out of yourself. Later I would figure out that the Army—the military in general— did not make anything out of you that you weren't already. So I went to the Army looking forward to the travel, the adventure, and whatever else a naive seventeen-year-old guy could get out of the Army service. Then, almost a year after I'd enlisted, Iraq invaded Kuwait. Like many hundreds of thousands of others, I soon found myself in the sands of Saudi Arabia waiting for the "mother of all battles" to begin.

While I was deployed, I learned to hide parts of myself from others. I began to learn how to dodge questions, or throw off suspicion. I became very good at this game, a game that so many of us would learn to play. And later, when "Don't Ask, Don't Tell" came along, I further honed my ability to live in the gray area. I learned to not get too close to people. People perceived me as stuck up.

The older I got, the more I realized I could not hide who I was. I was not going to be that guy who made up stories about some nonexistent girlfriend, nor was I going to date girls just to cover up for being gay.

When I finally did open up and come out to people, some were put off that I hadn't trusted them sooner. Many also told me they'd suspected I was gay anyway. It made me think of all the friendships I missed out on by not being open, all the people I could have educated by just being me.

I am glad repeal has finally come. I sincerely hope the next generation of soldiers will live free of all the smoke-and-mirror tricks we were once compelled to use just for the chance to serve our country in a military that would not have us the way we are.

Jeff Mueller is a developmental engineer
in the U.S. Air Force. He is currently stationed
at Schriever Air Force Base, Colorado,
working for the Missile Defense Agency.

While I was in training in California I befriended a gay civilian named Mike*. Mike and another friend, Sara*, and I hung out together all the time. We did everything together. I was never interested in Mike romantically, but it was just nice to have a friend I could be myself around. He had grown up in the central coast of California and had some other friends in the military—or so he said.

A few months into our friendship, Mike told me that he had a friend in OSI—the Air Force Office of Special Investigations—and that I was under investigation for being gay. I was terrified. I had not even been in the Air Force for a year, and already I thought I was going to be kicked out. Mike put me in contact with his friend that worked for OSI. Actually, his friend hacked into my Hotmail account and sent me an e-mail from my own account. He told me that I should watch what I post on the Internet and that my password was way too easy to hack. I was terrified now, but there really wasn't anything I could do. I trusted Mike and asked him for all the information on the investigation that he could find out.

He told me he found out that one of my oldest friends, Laura*, had called in and reported me to OSI in retaliation for an argument we'd had. He said my file was on a major's desk in OSI at the Air Force base where I was training at the time. His contact in OSI told me that it was at the bottom of the pile, but still I spent every day looking over my shoulder, wondering if today would be the day I got kicked out of the Air Force. I confronted my friend Laura about exposing me and she vehemently denied doing so. She even went so far as to fax me a copy of her phone records to prove that she hadn't made the call. I still did not believe her.

Soon after, I left California for my first real assignment, at Malmstrom Air Force Base, in Great Falls, Montana. Once there, I still talked to Mike and his OSI contact. I had not talked to Laura since she'd faxed me her phone bill. Mike's friend told me the file had followed me to Montana, where it was still in someone's inbox. I could not believe it.

As time wore on, I thought less about it as I started a new life. I began to make a group of friends and was having a great time in Great Falls. Mike decided that he wanted to move to Montana. I told him he could stay with me while he looked for a place to live. He stayed with me for about three weeks. Things were different now; I had a different group of friends and was not hanging out with him all the time. Mike started dating a guy who I'd met online and was slightly interested in. He became very possessive and wanted me to spend all my time with him, but eventually he got his own apartment and moved out. He lasted another few months before moving back to California. We continued to talk, but not as often. I eventually started to meet some other gay military guys in Montana, and it was nice to have a group of friends who could relate.

One of my friends knew someone who worked for OSI at Malmstrom. I asked him to check to see if there was a file on me. Nothing. There was no file and there never had been. I was in shock. A year of my life spent looking over my shoulder, paranoid that I was going to get kicked out, and losing one of my best friends. It was all made up, the entire story. Mike wanted me for himself and used the one thing he knew would drive away those that threatened his chances with me: my career. I eventually called my friend Laura and apologized to her. Our friendship had been damaged, all because I'd trusted someone who was screwing with me over someone who was a dear friend, and it all turned out to be a big lie. He used "Don't Ask, Don't Tell" to jealously pit me against my friends for his own personal gain. A law that had nothing to do with my performance as an Air Force officer, but instead who I loved, and it created a year of my life I will never forget.

Chad Diers* currently serves in the U.S. Navy.

I remember it like it was yesterday. I was on watch in the pilot house, and over a period of about forty-five minutes my three closest friends made a total of five visits to let me know that someone on the ship was spreading rumors that I was a "fag." My thoughts flashed back to stories I had heard about my dad getting jumped and beaten while on deployment to Europe for suspicion of being gay. Here I was, years later, finding myself in the same place, thousands of miles from home, with no family, no gay friends to relate to, and an extremely limited number of people I could talk to for comfort and support. It was the longest watch I ever stood, as thoughts about my safety, or lack thereof, ran through my mind. I was concerned not solely about my physical safety, but about my job, my life's career, as well. For all I knew, I could be brought up on charges, discharged, and abandoned somewhere abroad. I didn't know how discharges worked while overseas and I was quite frightened to find out.

That night I didn't sleep. I went topside and sat up on the

weather decks. The sky was pitch black and the clouds obscured the moon and stars; it definitely didn't help the loneliness and isolation I was feeling. I'm not sure how many hours I sat up there sorting through things; I just knew I had to get away and be alone.

The next day I ran into the guy responsible for the rumors. My heart skipped a beat and I had this strangling feeling in my throat. I pulled him aside and told him I needed to talk to him. With my hand clenched in a fist, I threatened him. I told him that everything he was saying about me was untrue and unproven and I told him that if he didn't stop spreading his stories I was going to take him to captain's mast so quick his head would spin. I let him know I would do everything I could to make sure he was brought up on charges. I was terrified. The whole time I thought for sure he could see me trembling. I was backed into a corner and doing the only thing I knew I could do. I had to put an end to these "untruths."

Weeks went by with me waiting and wondering, not knowing if I was going to be called into an office to have my sexuality questioned and my dignity stripped, or if this would all blow over. It was that night that I first realized this wasn't going to be the easiest career path for me.

Nothing ever came of it—no charges, no questioning from my superiors, and thankfully no discharge. But I was resolved to never go through that sort of ordeal again.

A few years later I married a woman. I would no longer have to lie about why I didn't have a girlfriend, why I didn't want to go out and pick up chicks. I would finally have a name to drop instead of playing the pronoun game. Yet it is all a lie. I am not proud that I felt I had to get married in order to serve in the military, but I consider it a small price to pay to allow me to serve without the constant anguish of having my sexuality questioned or wondering what rumors are being spread behind my back.

With the recent repeal of DADT, I know I can finally get a divorce and not worry so much about losing everything, or having so many years of service thrown into the trash. Still, I am not sure. Is this something I can do? I've grown very accustomed to the ring that has protected me over the years. It's become a part of who I am, yet it is also a reminder of the daily lies I've been forced to tell. Maybe it's time to take it off my finger, but now doing so is about as hard as it was to put it on in the first place.

Jeffrey Priela is a petty officer second class and hospital corpsman in the U.S. Navy currently stationed in Hawaii. He has been on active duty for over five years and has been deployed multiple times. He is the current chapter leader of OutServe Hawaii.

On my first ship there was a sailor, Dee, who practically flaunted his gayness. There were constant rumors spread about him. But the one saving grace for Dee was that he knew every facet of his job. He was a favorite of the commanding officer, and this professional alliance saved him from the many who would have liked to see him drummed out of the Navy for his "indiscretions."

One day, on one of the restroom stalls, I came across a very crudely written phrase that was directly addressed to Dee. Several more disparaging remarks were made against two or three other gay members on the ship. It was time to make a stand. I took my digital camera and snapped a few shots. I then gave it to our chief, who just so happened to be the equal opportunity officer on the ship. But he also happened to be Dee's biggest critic—he would constantly find some excuse to criticize the sailor.

My chief made some vague promise to do something about the harassment, but it was obvious that he was not going to take a stand. I decided to share the evidence with Dee as well, in the hope that he might show the photos to his ally, the commanding officer.

Thirty minutes later, a booming voice came over the loudspeaker of the ship.

It was the commanding officer.

He shouted that he did not want to see this kind of behavior on his ship again. It is not a person's sexual orientation that drives the ship, he said, it is the sailor's ability to go above and beyond the call of duty. He even threatened all personnel and Marines that our free time off the ship would be restricted if the incident was repeated.

It was an indescribable moment. I felt a swelling of pride in my chest. My respect for the commanding officer increased tenfold. And for a few short minutes, I felt that Dee had been vindicated.

Still, I knew that this small victory did not mean that we were now free from discrimination. In the next year I enjoyed tremendous success. I was well recognized for my work and was promoted several times. In time, everyone in my division and ship learned that I was gay, but I didn't speak openly about it. I focused more on my professional life. Success was my strategy for combating homophobia.

During difficult times on the ship, when I needed to be alone, I spent a tremendous amount of time in a storage closet on board. It was cramped, but despite the discomfort, it was a place of solitude and security. There, I quite literally had my own room on board this ship. It's where I would go when I wanted to get away, to meditate, or at times cry.

It was there in that cold and unforgiving closet that I began to truly investigate my sexual orientation. I could be my true self, with no fear, while alone there, but as soon as I walked out I had to leave everything inside. In this private space I learned that not all closets are bad after all. But I look forward to the day when they won't be necessary, when gay sailors will be free to serve with total openness.

Stephen McCrory is a second lieutenant in the
U.S. Air Force currently stationed at
Keesler Air Force Base, Mississippi.

G reg and I worked together, but we didn't really become close until mutual friends introduced us to each other while we were out one night. We immediately clicked; once we started talking we never quite stopped. For the next year we spent almost all of our spare time together: dinner at one of the dining facilities on base, activities off base, traveling around the area, video games in his dorm room—normal things that friends do. We often spent whole evenings quietly hanging out, Greg on his computer on one side of the room, me reading a book on the other side of the room. Maybe twenty words, a handful of sentences would pass between us. "What book is that?"

"Stephen King's *Eyes of the Dragon.* How's that new game?"

"Not bad."

An hour later:

"Wanna watch a movie?"

"Yup. You choose."

We were immediately comfortable in each other's presence.

Many months passed this way before I realized that I might be romantically interested in Greg.

I don't know exactly when I fell in love, or how I came to realize that I cared more for him than anyone I'd ever known outside of my family. This did not, however, bode well for me. Greg was engaged, had been since the day we met.

We continued to spend time together, with my feelings growing and Greg unaware. There was no need for me to express anything. We were fine, comfortable, close, platonically intimate. I had been through entirely too many rock-bottom, unrequited-love tragedies in the past with straight men, and I wasn't looking forward to another one.

Please, God, not another one. I love him too much.

I had promised Greg I would attend his wedding, but now I was having misgivings. I spoke to a chaplain, who told me that just as people should accept me for who I am, so should I. What a ton of bricks that was. As an act of catharsis, I decided to attend, and was pleasantly surprised when Greg asked me to be a groomsman. But there was still a deep and abiding longing—a desire that something, anything would happen and I wouldn't have to face the overwhelming loss and grief. I also came to truly care for Greg's beautiful wife, and with that new friendship came horrible guilt about my feelings for Greg.

I cried long and hard when I left the wedding. I can only describe the sadness as simultaneously exquisite and excruciating. I couldn't sleep. I couldn't eat. Everything had him in it.

Over the next several weeks, my higher-ups approached me one by one and asked what was going on. They expressed genuine concern, which gave me something to be thankful for. At one point even my flight commander said to me, "What's going on? You've just seemed . . . *distraught*." But I was too afraid to tell them exactly what was going on. How could I, with the policies in place at the time?

I was overcome with contradictory feelings. I felt like I should not be feeling this way, should not sacrifice my happiness, should not sacrifice my career, should not still love him.

My only recourse at the time for professional help was a chaplain—a different one, as the other had moved on. After listening to my predicament, this new chaplain basically told me that if I could fix this gay part of me, everything would be fine.

Wow. I'd not thought of that. Let me just reach inside myself and flip this switch real quick—wait, where . . . ? Oh, that's right. It doesn't work like that. I love our chaplains and respect and support the work they do, but this was downright insulting. So now my choices were suffer alone, leave the service, or turn my gay switch to the off position. A rather bleak situation, if you ask me.

I have since come to live with the fact that Greg and I are not meant to be together and never will be. We are still close friends.

His wife is a beautiful person and I am glad to be a part of their lives, and to have witnessed something as momentous as their union before God and man. I will always consider them an extension of my family.

Countless soldiers have experienced unrequited love, and my heartbreak was no different from theirs. The only difference was that my feelings for Greg could have gotten me ousted from the military.

Danny Hernandez was a lance corporal in the
U.S. Marine Corps. Since his separation from
the Marines he has been a staff member at
Servicemembers Legal Defense Network,
where he has worked for the repeal of
"Don't Ask, Don't Tell."

At the beginning of my senior year in high school, a Marine recruiter called me and asked if I had any interest in joining. I had been researching my options for after high school, and assumed that I would attend a private Christian school in Texas. As the oldest of nine kids, however, I wondered how was I going to pay for school. The military seemed like a good option.

When I met with the recruiter in the fall of 2004, I was a naive seventeen-year-old kid. He couldn't have been more disgusted with me. I know this because he in fact told me himself. At five feet, two inches, I weighed a mere eighty-five pounds and was able to do one complete pull-up.

One.

But I was ranked at the top of my graduating class, and my recruiter remained impressed with my capabilities outside of athleticism. He gave me a workout routine and committed his efforts to helping me become a good Marine. He motivated me and called me his "prodigy." Soon thereafter, I fell in love with the Corps.

Months later, after gaining some weight and strength, I signed the paperwork, took the oath, and received a ship date for boot camp. As the date approached, I worked diligently in my last year of high school and in preparation for my next few years as a Marine. One day, however, my recruiter took me aside and told me something I would have never expected to hear from a recruiter. He advised me to drop my enlistment contract and consider going to college in pursuit of an officer commission. This surprised me, but made me realize I was lucky: my recruiter had my best interests in mind.

I began college at Texas A&M. During my third year, I decided to enlist in the active Marine Reserves. The passion I had before college had remained, and after three years of Reserve Officer Training Corps (ROTC) and the Corps of Cadets, I was more than prepared for success at boot camp. My plan at this point was to do my training, then return to school as a reservist, graduate college, switch to active duty, and commission as an officer after I had relevant experience under my belt. After training I returned to A&M for my senior year in the fall of 2008 able to call myself a United States Marine for the very first time.

During college I had become more comfortable with my sexuality. When I joined the ROTC at seventeen, I wasn't sure who I was, but over time I came to understand that I was gay. I told a few close friends, most of them buddies from the Corps of Cadets, but was by no means "out." There was never a negative issue that arose because of my sexuality. After I graduated I planned to begin active duty in pursuit of an officer commission. "Don't Ask, Don't Tell" didn't factor into my decisions at all.

In the spring of my senior year in college, however, I confronted the reality of DADT. It started one night when I went out with some friends to a local bar. I was with a lot of people, a few who knew I was gay and some who did not. Among the latter was a group of Marines that I didn't know personally, but were hanging out with us while they pursued some girls in our group. It came up in conversation that I was gay, and at first it was shrugged off. But after a while the Marines began heckling us and making inappropriate comments toward both me and the girls. They then became aggressive. I stood up for myself, and for the girls, but soon we all left. In the days that followed, I worried that the Marines at the bar would tell my command chain about my sexual orientation.

I became so worried that I eventually talked to a corporal I felt comfortable with. I told him what had happened, and in doing so revealed that I was gay. He then told my platoon sergeant. We all talked, and, to my surprise, they calmed me down, reassured me that it was not a big deal. To them, the only thing that mattered was that I got to the unit for weekend drill. I went to drill as instructed, but when I arrived I learned that my story had spread, reaching my first sergeant and commanding officer. Two Marine friends who knew I was gay were asked to provide written statements, and they complied. This led to the first investigation.

When I walked into my first sergeant's office, the first thing he asked me was, "Are you gay?" It was immediately a hostile environment. I hesitated, but answered honestly. He proceeded to tell me that there was no way he could protect my privacy, he could not stop the "grapevine," and he could not stop what people within the unit said or did. When I met with my commanding officer later the same day, he went over the events with me, explaining why I should be discharged. But I wasn't told what my fate would be. I was simply told to "hang tight" and wait on what the battalion commander would say.

I was now worried about how I was going to be treated by my unit after the investigation. I did not feel safe and I did not know who to contact or talk to. I wasn't out to my family, and my pride kept me from talking to my friends from college. I was alone. I waited and waited on a status update and did not hear anything for months. Ultimately, I contacted a friend from the unit and asked him to find out my status. He got back to me about a week later and informed me that I was discharged from the Marine Corps in April 2010. My commander finally notified me officially shortly afterward.

I look at pictures from my short time in the Marine Corps Reserve and wonder where I would be at this point if it hadn't been for "Don't Ask, Don't Tell." Would I be commissioned? Would I be overseas? I don't know the answer, but I do know that, despite my setback, I still look forward to the day when I can proudly wear the uniform again. I made a commitment to my country and I intend to honor it.

Anthony "Andy" Blevins was a petty officer
second class and cryptologic technician in the
U.S. Navy from 2007 to 2011. Stationed at the
Naval Computer and Telecommunications Station
in Guam, he served as the command's information
assurance officer and facilities control officer.

I grew up in a fairly religious household, we went to church twice a week, and it was well known in our household that homosexuals go to hell. I joined the Navy to prove to myself that I was not gay. In my mind at the time, all gay men were spitting images of Richard Simmons or Ru Paul. In my mind, gay men could not survive in the military.

I left for boot camp thirty days after my eighteenth birthday. From basic training, I headed to the Naval Nuclear Power Training Command in Charleston, South Carolina. I made several friends, and one drunken night confessed to a female friend that I thought I was gay. She told me about another gay friend of hers in the military. He became my first "real" boyfriend. Our toxic relationship was short-lived—I can never remember what ended it—but I will never forget how spiteful he was. He went to our chain of command with fabricated evidence that I tried to rape him. I was crushed. How could somebody that I'd cared so much about do something so terrible? Charges were eventually dropped, as there was no proof of anything.

But after that I wasn't the same. I had nobody to talk to, for fear of losing my career. My friends, the chaplain, my chain of command—they were all out of the question. I resorted to putting myself through a program at one of the local churches to "cure" myself of being gay. I spent most of my days repeating the rosary, praying, and fasting—all punishments for my "evil" behavior. I would cry myself to sleep. I exiled myself from my family and friends. All because I was scared. I was scared I was going to hell. I was scared to be alone. I was scared because I wasn't happy with myself.

The program lasted for eight weeks. There was a little graduation ceremony on the last day. After you got your diploma, you were set up on a date with a member of the opposite sex from the class. I was set up with Sara. We went to an Italian restaurant, a recommendation from our program instructor. The night started off incredibly awkwardly. We had nothing to talk about. Luckily, we saw another couple from our class, so we decided to invite them over—a double date. Things went great. We sat at the table for almost four hours, laughing, cracking jokes, talking about everything and anything. Once we'd said our awkward good-byes to our dates, I headed home for the night. When I arrived home, I couldn't stop smiling. I was on top of the world, thinking about how well my double date had gone. As I was settling in for bed still mulling the night over in my head, my stomach suddenly dropped. I realized I wasn't thinking about Sara at all. I was thinking about John, the other guy on our double date. I felt sick. My head started spinning. I'd failed the program. I hated myself.

It took a while, but eventually I came to terms with being gay. I no longer viewed the Navy as a tool to assert my manliness, or to prove I was straight. But others weren't so lucky. Since I've been a sailor, two very close friends of mine, both gay, took their own lives.

"Don't Ask, Don't Tell" not only prevented our loved ones, and spouses, from receiving the benefits and rights that their hetero-sexual counterparts received—benefits and rights that my husband, Heath, never received—but it prevented gay and lesbian service members from receiving the help they needed. It prevented them from being able to say, "Hey, I'm really scared right now, Chaplain. Can we talk about this?" The policy fostered a poisonous environment, one in which service members—willing to die for the rights of this great nation—were forced to lie and compromise their personal integrity.

To all the gay and lesbian service members past and present, I salute you. I salute you for the anguish you imposed on yourself. I salute you for the turmoil others imposed on you. I salute you for the countless nights you lay awake crying. I salute you for your desire to serve our great nation. Let us always remember the words of former U.S. senator Barry Goldwater: "You don't have to be straight to be in the military; you just have to be able to shoot straight."

Katherine "Katie" Miller was a cadet at West Point
until she resigned in protest of "Don't Ask, Don't
Tell." She worked as one of OutServe's main
spokespersons during the fight to repeal DADT,
appearing on national television and escorting
Lady Gaga at MTV's Music Video Awards.
She is currently studying at Yale and serves
on OutServe's board of directors.

I sat in the cadet mess hall for mandatory dinner after returning to West Point grounds following a summer of military training. I couldn't bring myself to eat anything more than a dinner roll, my stomach was contorted into knots. I had submitted a memorandum to my commander the day prior, entitled "Written Statement of Resignation and Formal Disclosure of Homosexual Orientation." I would be discharged from the U.S. Military Academy in three days' time.

I slipped away unnoticed from the table, returned to my empty transient barracks room, and logged on to my GI computer. I had only a couple minutes to prepare. I was about to discuss my resignation on national television. Everything I had kept a secret was now going to be broadcast live.

I had just put on my dress-white uniform, freshly pinned with my new cadet sergeant rank, when I heard the jiggling of my doorknob turning. My best friend entered without a word and gently pushed the door closed behind her. She examined me up and down, observing my tightly pulled-back hair, my beltline, and finally my shoes. She grabbed my shirt and tugged downward, prompting me to tuck it into my trousers even more tightly than it already was. "You're ready," she declared.

A moment later I heard that familiar jiggling again, and three other friends walked in. They informed me that another friend was outside guarding the door. I hadn't expected to see any of them. Knowing fully what I was getting myself into, several days earlier I had warned them against being seen with me. I was afraid they might be accused themselves if they were associated with me.

The room was again quiet until the soft ring of a Skype call interrupted. It was the producer from *The Rachel Maddow Show*. It was time. My best friend handed me a "Beat Navy!" towel to wipe the beads of sweat from my forehead. I sat down to face the computer camera. The producer fell silent and the booming voice of Rachel Maddow emerged. "Cadet Miller, tell me what it's like to have been at West Point with this policy in place, and why you have decided to resign." To this day I can't recall how I responded. What

I do remember is staring into that screen, revealing emotions and experiences I had fiercely guarded for years to an audience whose vastness I couldn't possibly fathom.

Seven minutes later I logged off my computer and didn't dare glance at my huddled friends opposite me in the room. I heard one let out a sigh as another squeezed my shoulder firmly. I changed out of the formal uniform into the Army camouflage everyone else was wearing, and marched alongside them to a secluded area outside. Realizing the irreversibility of my actions and that I would be indefinitely ineligible for military service, I suddenly felt great disdain for myself. "I took the easy way out," I said to my friends. "It's not fair that I'll be a civilian soon, and you'll still be here living with the policy, fighting for me and the rest of the country despite the additional burden. I should be with you."

"No," my friend responded, "you'll be out there fighting for *me*. You'll be doing something I don't have the power to do. You're still doing your duty—it just looks a little different." She added, "Plus, we all know you'll be back anyway." I finally smiled.

I returned to my room alone. In that moment I knew that coming out and speaking out wasn't about me anymore. It was about my friends, my comrades. It was about them and all those who had come before us and who will come after us. It was—just like the United States Military Academy class of 2012 motto states—for a cause "greater than ourselves."

W e are not a nation that says, 'Don't Ask, Don't Tell.'
We are a nation that says, 'Out of many, we are one.' We
are a nation that welcomes the service of every patriot.
We are a nation that believes all men and women are
created equal. Those are the ideals that generations have
fought for. Those are the ideals we uphold today."

—President Barack Obama, at
the signing ceremony for the DADT Repeal Act,
December 22, 2010

Tania Dunbar is a warrant officer in the U.S. Army.
She was deployed in Iraq at the time of writing this,
and is currently stationed in Georgia.

I have been in the Army for almost twelve years. My very first day in basic training, I knew I had found my calling. I also knew that I was gay, and I wasn't supposed to be there. My recruiter had made me sign a piece of paper saying I was not gay, had never had sex with anyone of the same sex, and had never attempted to marry anyone of the same sex. I signed it because I did not understand the extent to which the Army was going to make me hide a part of myself.

For the past eleven years I have had to conceal my family from my friends. Soldiers, with whom I sweat, bleed, and cry, can't ever meet the woman I love. Soldiers who depend on me for sound judgment and advice can never know who I myself go to when I need advice or solace. Friends who would die for me can't ever meet the person who makes me want to live. Don't get me wrong—there are a few soldiers who know I am gay, but it takes a long time to learn if you can trust someone with a secret that can ruin your career. So I don't make friends easily, I never have get-togethers at my home, and I don't go to military functions very often. For me, home life cannot mix with work life.

I am in Iraq now, separated from the love of my life, and I can't share that pain with anyone. If I am hurt or I die while in combat here, my girlfriend will not be notified. She wouldn't even be able to visit me in the hospital. We have to depend on an intricate web of lies and code words to get us through a year of separation. I find it strange to think that I am in a foreign country, making sure that other people are able to exercise their democratic rights, ensuring that they get their basic civil rights—to life, liberty, and happiness— while I don't get those same basic rights. And yet our allies allow homosexuals to serve openly in their militaries; they are deployed with us, and enjoy full rights.

Department of Defense Directive 5120.36, issued in July 1963 by Secretary of Defense Robert McNamara, clearly states: "Every military commander has the responsibility to oppose discriminatory practices affecting his men and their dependents and to foster equal opportunity for them, not only in areas under his immediate control, but also in nearby communities where they may live or gather in off-duty hours."

That directive was issued to deal directly with racism in areas surrounding military communities fifteen years after Executive Order 9981, in which President Truman ordered the military to integrate. It was an obvious example of the military righting a wrong, just as the repeal of "Don't Ask, Don't Tell" will be. The message—that military leaders have a responsibility to create an environment of tolerance and equality—is the same.

I love the Army and I love my girlfriend, and I should not have to choose between them. I volunteered to sacrifice my life for this country, but I can't even hug my girlfriend good-bye before I deploy. You have asked me to deploy twice to protect other people in other countries. You have asked me to stand vigil against terrorists in our country. I am asking the same from you now: I am asking you to treat me equally, protect me from injustice, and help me when others try to hurt me.

*Anthony Loverde was a staff sergeant and
loadmaster for the C-130 in the U.S. Air Force until
he resigned under "Don't Ask, Don't Tell."*

I was a loadmaster on C-130 aircraft, the head of a six-man crew working together executing cargo missions in and out of Iraq. This was a special crew, and working with these incredibly talented people strengthened my sense of duty toward my fellow man. I would do anything for them, and I know they would do the same for me. Unfortunately, "Don't Ask, Don't Tell" caused me to build barriers. I couldn't share anything about my personal life with them. I avoided them so much after our missions that they nicknamed me "Vapor," because I would disappear as soon as we hit the ground.

Our crew was a diverse group: Five males, two females. Four married, three single. Six heterosexual, one homosexual. One Jew, one Christian, one atheist, and four who didn't share their religious affiliations. Needless to say, this diversity sparked some interesting conversations while we were at cruising altitude. Everyone would share stories of home and what they missed the most. They shared their dreams for the future, and told what they'd like to do together when we all got back. Except for me. I had to avoid all personal questions. I couldn't fully take part in any of the normal conversations—about relationships, family life, the future—that crew members had as they tried to get to know one another, build trust, and create a common bond.

I was well aware of DADT, but also felt it was wrong to mislead my crewmembers. I had too much respect for my fellow crew members to lie to them. Still, I was forced to avoid the truth. Yet they suspected I was gay. There were signs—I read gay-themed books and my mannerisms may have been a tip off. Once, when asked what kind of woman I was attracted to, I answered, "I like women with broad shoulders, thick thighs, deep voices—and the hairier the better." I tried to tell the truth through humor.

But it weighed heavily on my conscience that there was no way of truthfully answering the questions my friends were asking. It also became increasingly difficult to deal with my homophobic supervisor. He once approached me on a mission to order me to move a civilian that he suspected to be a "faggot" to the opposite side of the aircraft because he didn't want to sit next to any "faggot." At the time, he didn't know he was speaking to a "faggot" and it would have been impossible for me to let him know that his behavior was inappropriate. Instead, I was forced to politely ask the civilian to sit in a different area of the aircraft.

One morning, during routine inspection for flight, the crew chief noticed one of the books I'd brought with me to read during flight. He asked to see it, then read the back cover, which mentioned that the author was the editor of *Gay City News*. "The author is a faggot?" the crew chief asked. "If you mean homosexual," I replied, "then, yes, I do believe he is." I also let the crew chief know that the author was a personal friend of mine. The crew chief then explained that his best friend at home was a "fag," and didn't mind him using the word "fag." I let him know that most gay people don't like to be referred to as "fags." The crew chief was a black man, and I told him that the word was as derogatory as using the n-word. He said he understood.

I began to realize that my censorship of my private life was too unbearable to live with for the remainder of my career. I decided halfway through my deployment that when I returned to my home station in Germany, I would come out to my commander in hopes of gaining his support to serve openly with future crews. To be open and honest with my crew would be fair to all, including me: denying the truth was no longer acceptable. I dealt with the discomfort for the rest of the deployment and my crew continued to work well together, even though their suspicions about my sexuality didn't flag.

When we finished our deployment and returned to Germany, I finally got up the courage to send an e-mail to my first sergeant and commander stating we needed to talk about my desire to no longer follow the "Don't Ask, Don't Tell" policy. This e-mail spurred my discharge. My crew was in my corner the entire time, supporting and encouraging me. Now that repeal has come, they're all asking me when I plan to come back.

*Michelle Benecke, Esq., served as a captain
and battery commander in the U.S. Army.
She is a founder and former executive director
of Servicemembers Legal Defense Network,
the pioneering legal aid and policy organization
for gays and lesbians in the military. Michelle is
a graduate of the University of Virginia
and Harvard Law School.*

I served as an Army officer and battery commander in the 1980s. This was a time when women were being integrated into the all-male, nontraditional fields of the military, like Air Defense Artillery, in which I served. At the time, I was told there were about twenty-six of us women officers in a branch of fifty-five thousand men.

I was one of few women to lead combat arms soldiers, in my case with a contingency mission to southwest Asia—Afghanistan, Pakistan, Iran, and surrounding areas. I was not afraid of being called on to fight for our country. Every day, however, I lived in fear of being found out as gay and suffering an end to my career. Being in the military was much more than a job—for me, it was a calling, an identity, community, duty, and honor.

Along the way, I became one of only ten Army officers selected for a fully funded fellowship to law school. This was a prestigious program, with a guarantee of plum assignments afterward and promotion to the highest ranks. Ultimately, however, I made the painful decision to resign my commission as a military officer and forfeit that fellowship because of the military's ban on homosexuals. I could not come back and prosecute other gay people, nor could I continue to live a double life and lie every day about who I was. I believed in the military's core values of honesty and integrity—still do. The military's bans were antithetical to those values.

This was an era in which witch hunts were rampant. The military's criminal investigators led these investigations. With their resources and global reach, one allegation could be leveraged into a wide-ranging dragnet.

The majority of women serving in my branch were investigated as suspected lesbians at one time or another, regardless of their actual sexual orientation. I was no exception. One month before leaving the military, after I had already turned in my resignation, investigators from the Army's Criminal Investigative Division, or CID, came into my barracks at night, without informing my first sergeant. They pulled two soldiers down to CID and proceeded to interrogate them. My soldiers were pressured to accuse me of being gay and to lodge false allegations that I had made unwanted advances toward them. They refused to do so. One of them was also questioned about her own sexual orientation.

I ultimately survived the investigation, although it was a terrifying time. I had been accepted to Harvard Law School and had already vowed to start an advocacy group for members of the military once I was out of the service. Until the investigation was closed, however, the Army would not release me. When I was finally released, it was a bittersweet moment. I barely made it to Harvard in time to start law school.

It wasn't until I began researching and writing at law school that I realized the gay ban was being used across all services, not only in my branch of the Army as a way to rout women out of nontraditional fields. A law school classmate and I also began to document its retaliatory use against women who reported sexual harassment. In our first year at law school, Kirstin Dodge and I published a law journal piece many still consider to be the seminal work on how and why the military's antigay policies were used disproportionately against women. Other publications followed. They were circulated within the military, and from that time on I began taking calls from military members who needed assistance. These experiences only strengthened my resolve to start that advocacy group.

"Don't Ask, Don't Tell" was supposed to stop the witch hunts and other abuses. The day after its passage into law, the phones began ringing off the hook at the Campaign for Military Service, the umbrella organization that had originally tried to lift the ban on gays in the armed forces. Military members were calling for help because the witch hunts had immediately started back up.

Dixon Osburn, whom I had met at CMS, was as concerned as I. No existing organization was interested in pursuing repeal of "Don't Ask, Don't Tell," or was able to assist members of the military who were being affected by it. In the short window of opportunity we had, we formed Servicemembers Legal Defense Network. SLDN became the pioneering legal aid and policy organization for gays and lesbians in uniform, and, in 1993, launched the long-term effort to repeal "Don't Ask, Don't Tell." SLDN has helped thousands of Americans whose livelihoods were put in jeopardy by the discriminatory policy.

To this day Servicemembers Legal Defense Network continues to fight for the equality of LGBT service members, such as those who are still not able to get married and are subject to workplace discrimination, or veterans who want to receive upgrades on their previous discharges for "homosexual conduct." A tremendous amount of progress has been made, but there is still a lot of work to do.

Scott Konzem is a captain and C-17 pilot in the U.S. Air Force. He is currently stationed at McGuire Air Force Base, New Jersey.

As an active duty C-17 pilot, my job requires extensive periods of travel—sometimes in the form of deployments, but most times in the form of trips lasting ten to twenty days. It's difficult enough to keep in touch and remain emotionally engaged given this sort of schedule, but adding "Don't Ask, Don't Tell" into the equation has made the challenge even greater for countless same-sex couples.

Communication while on the road is a serious challenge. "Morale phones" aren't easily available, and trying to have a censored conversation makes conversation more difficult still. Initially, I would try to keep my conversations brief and brotherly, so that anyone listening in would think I was talking to a family member instead of my partner. I couldn't say "I miss you" or "I love you" for fear of being monitored or overheard. Using any sort of e-mail or chat programs over the government computer network also made me very leery, because there are people whose job is to monitor communication. I understand they aren't necessarily hunting for gays, but the fear was always there that the wrong person could read the wrong e-mail and report me. As a result, my partner and I found it difficult to remain emotionally engaged, and the time I've spent away has been the most difficult in our relationship.

At some point, I broke down and bought a worldwide cell phone so that we could text like normal people in a relationship without fear of being monitored. It's all about the little things, and being able to say "I love you" or "I'm going crazy without you" can make all the difference in the world. Then, about two years into the demanding travel schedule, I also gave up on trying to censor myself over government communication sources. I stopped caring—it wasn't worth the stress to our relationship to constantly live in fear of Big Brother discovering our illegal and supposedly immoral relationship. It's not like we were being graphic or pornographic anyway; we simply needed to communicate like everyone else.

The second challenge is on the home front for my partner. The Air Force has a great spouse network (or "spouse mafia," as we call them) that provides support and encouragement during the hard times. It's important for a person to feel like they're not alone, and the spouse mafia does a great job at providing that support. Unfortunately, because our relationship has been forbidden, my partner has had no support. He has had to deal with everything a military spouse has to deal with, from loneliness to prolonged periods with no contact, alone. The way my partner handles this situation is a testament to his strength and inner fortitude. It's not the sort of thing anyone should ever have to face alone—yet he does. No matter how miserable my situation is overseas, I always tell myself, "I chose this career." Although my partner chose to be with a military man, his choice was not quite the same as mine. I know his own friends do all they can to help him through the difficult times, but nobody really understands what it's like unless you've been through it yourself.

I also feel isolated when I'm away from home. It gets old having to put on the straight act day after day. When I'm not deployed, I don't have to keep up the charade twenty-four/seven—at the end of the day I can go home and be myself. But at some point, this got to be too much. My sexuality has never dominated my personality, but after months of having to lie all the time, I began to feel frustrated and lonely. I was never lucky enough to deploy with other gay service members, so I didn't have others I could be myself around.

I eventually gave up—all the lying was making me crazy. I started violating "Don't Ask, Don't Tell" and told coworkers who were close to me. I was moved and encouraged by the reactions of my peers, who all continued to love and support me. Finally I could have an honest conversation. The fact that no one had any issues with my sexuality was tremendously encouraging and suggests to me that there won't be many serious issues in the postrepeal era.

All we can do is hope it continues to get better. Maybe some religious zealots will still have a problem with who I am—someday I hope they'll see the light too—but at least the government-sanctioned violation of my rights has begun to stop. I look forward to a world in which my partner and I will feel like we are part of the same military community as everyone else, and in which who I am will elevate rather than threaten my career. My hope is that the DADT repeal is just the beginning—that it will serve to open other doors, finally bringing an end to other legalized discrimination, such as the Defense of Marriage Act.

Ryan Quinn is a captain and C-17 pilot in the
U.S. Air Force. He is currently stationed at
McGuire Air Force Base, New Jersey.

I have been through many lonely times in my life, but none quite so lonely as the time I spent at the Air Force Academy. I don't mean to say that every moment was bad. Of course there were a lot of good things about the academy. I had good times with my friends. I learned a lot about the Air Force, about being an officer, and about myself. But I also learned a lot about feeling very alone.

When I was a cadet at the academy, from June of 2000 to June of 2004, there weren't many ways for a gay kid to feel accepted. When I first started out, I had no clue if there was anybody there who might understand me. By the time I graduated, I was certain that nobody in the Air Force ever would.

There is one day in particular that sticks with me. It was a windy day in March, one of those days when the Colorado winter seems endless and the misery of the school year is at its worst. I was walking across campus after class, talking with my best friend.

I mentioned a fellow classmate who had said or done something that seemed "gay." When I suggested that the classmate might actually be gay, my friend disagreed. "I don't think that anyone at the academy is gay," he said. I asked him if he was sure, thinking how ironic it was that he was making this declaration to what might be the one gay kid in the whole place. Yes, he was pretty sure, he said, and continued to say he didn't think a gay person would survive at the academy. Of course, I knew he was wrong, because I was most definitely surviving. I pressed the issue, asking if he *really* believed that, out of forty-four hundred cadets, not a single one was gay? "They just wouldn't fit in here," he replied. On that score, sadly, he ended up being right.

After that conversation, I remember thinking how foolish I'd been to choose that school. Were my dreams of flying really worth the sacrifice I was making? Could I continue to live a life surrounded by people who didn't understand me, and probably wouldn't like the real me? My best friend didn't even understand who I really was, and there was no way I could tell him the truth. How could I ever expect to be happy in this Air Force?

Fortunately, and surprisingly, today things are completely different. The change started when I met someone in my squadron who is gay, and he introduced me to another gay guy in the squadron. And he introduced me to others. Still I am amazed by the way my circle of friends has exploded. I've had gay supervisors and gay subordinates, and I also have a lot of straight friends here who know I'm gay. I feel like I fit in. These days the gay kid feels like he's at home in the Air Force.

And now, thanks to outlets such as Facebook and OutServe, I know that wherever I go in the world I'll have a set of friends, people who will understand and support me. With the fall of "Don't Ask, Don't Tell," I feel confident and grateful that my country accepts my ability to serve, and that things will keep getting better. Unlike during my time at the Air Force Academy, I now find I am rarely lonely. I am surrounded by friends and coworkers who truly understand me.

Looking back, I'm glad I chose to attend the Air Force Academy, and I'm glad I stuck with it. Sure, it was a painful, lonely four years I'd prefer not to repeat. But I don't regret it and I wouldn't change it. If anything, I would have changed myself. I would have been more open with my friends and my classmates, and I would have been more confident in myself. I would have also been more confident in the Air Force. Now that I've given it a chance, I realize how surprisingly supportive my fellow airmen can be.

Laurie Arellano is in the Air Force Reserves,
currently assigned to the U.S. Air Force
Expeditionary Center as a public affairs officer.

Getting married to my wife was the turning point in my life and my career. It changed everything for me—I simultaneously achieved my dreams and nearly demolished my career. I never imagined something that was supposed to be such a happy occasion could just about send me off the deep end.

I first realized I was gay after nearly twenty years in the military. It made me happy to finally know who I was, and I wasn't scared about "Don't Ask, Don't Tell"—I really felt I could fly under the radar. I don't look or act like a stereotypical lesbian, and I'd previously been married and had children, so I didn't raise flags with people. I had relationships only with civilian women, because I felt that was safer for me, and I worked very hard to keep my lives separate. I never discussed my private life with my coworkers, and I didn't bring my girlfriends to the base or to any functions. I generally felt this was going to be the best way to finish my career and be who I truly was inside. But it felt like I was leading a double life in many ways. Things at work were very complicated. I work in public affairs and had to be prepared to discuss "Don't Ask, Don't Tell" cases when those who were dismissed went public with their stories and the media became involved. I saw a lot of cases that made me fearful of the DoD because it seemed like they were bullying these airmen. The cases I saw were all young enlisted women, though, which in some ways made me feel like I was a little "safer," because I was a major and nearly eligible for retirement.

Then I met up with an old friend who had also recently come out. We had so much in common and we immediately clicked. Before I knew it, we were having a long-distance relationship, and I knew this wasn't going to make me happy for much longer. I knew I was in love. I felt like I had finally achieved what everyone dreams of: love and happiness. It was a very healthy relationship; she was very supportive of my military career and never complained that I couldn't be out. She wanted me to be happy, and she knew being in the service made me happy. We decided to get married and move in together. So we eloped to Canada, where same-sex marriage is legal, and had a ceremony. I lived off base, so it was easy for her to move in with me. I felt so weird, though, because I couldn't talk about it and, worse, she was very much an outsider, completely on her own if something happened to me.

Eventually I became courageous enough to start bringing my wife on base, introducing her as my friend, or as my day care provider so she could attend my kids' sporting events and office functions with me. We were very careful never to look like we were more than friends. There were times I thought my commander may have known, or at least suspected, and I wished I could be honest with him—I felt like a liar, and being an officer in public affairs, my credibility was everything to me. Only a very trusted few of my coworkers knew.

Apparently somebody else knew, though, and about six months after we got married, I was outed and an investigation began. All the bullying I had seen as a public affairs officer suddenly became my own reality, and it was chilling watching my career flash before my eyes. But I wasn't scared. I felt like if I was going to have to go down, it was worth it to have gained the most amazing wife and partner out of it. She supported me every step of the way, and let the decision and the fight be mine. She was worth every tear I cried and every anxiety attack I suffered through the investigation.

Now I'm out. I was lucky—my investigation began right before repeal, and it was closed right after. By then, everyone had connected the dots that my "friend" was more than that, and that I had been investigated. Turns out, the vast majority didn't care anyway.

My one regret is that I wasn't able to come out myself, that someone else outed me. I am sorry someone else got to do that, and that I didn't get to share the joy of my marriage the way my heterosexual military friends do. Moving forward, however, I just feel a great sense of relief that I no longer have to lie.

Robert Campbell is a senior airman in the U.S. Air Force currently stationed at Minot Air Force Base, North Dakota.

I am currently an enlisted airman in the United States Air Force. I work at one of five missile alert facilities as a missile food specialist. Basically, I'm a chef far out in the vast farmland in North Dakota. The facility is about fifty miles from the closest town, so while we're here at work, all we have is each other for a full shift, normally ninety-six hours or four days.

I was sitting at work watching TV when I saw the vote to repeal DADT pass in Congress. I was ecstatic that the policy would finally be over, as were most of my friends. For the first time I felt I wanted to stay in the military. Many excited text messages and e-mails passed between my friends and me. I even talked to our facility manager about the milestone congressional vote. He didn't understand why it was such a big deal for me personally, but he could see that it was a big step forward and very long overdue.

I decided to call my mom to share the news. My relationship with my stepmother was the strongest bond I had. I would tell her anything without hesitation and without fear of judgment. I loved her more than anything. She had been in the Army for several years herself, and she was one of the biggest driving forces for my joining the military. She was also the only member of my family still in contact with me after I'd come out. As close as we were, I knew she would be as happy as I was to learn that DADT had been repealed.

But when I shared the news, her response was not at all what I'd been expecting. She told me she hoped it was all a mistake, that repeal hadn't actually happened, because she didn't think gays had any place in the military. "When I was deployed," she went on to say, "I didn't want a faggot out there with me. I didn't want to have to think about someone looking at me instead of watching for the attack." I had never heard more hurtful words. I defended myself, telling her she had to know that, when I was deployed, looking at hot guys was the last thing on my mind. She told me I was "different than most gays."

I quickly got off the phone and returned to work. I was so upset, so visibly troubled, that my facility manager came over to suggest I go take some time to get myself together. I was barely holding back a scream, and he could see it.

That was the last conversation I had with my stepmother. Since then, our relationship has consisted of a letter once a month. Only one letter, to say "How are you?" and "I'm fine." Nothing more. It really hurts to know I've lost the one and only supporter I had left in my family.

Gage Parrot is a cadet at the U.S. Air
Force Academy, where he is studying
Arabic and computer science.

My experience serving under "Don't Ask, Don't Tell" has surprised me. When I began basic training, I was terrified that my squadmates would find out I was gay, and so I was depressed at the prospect of ten to fifteen years of living in hiding. But by the time the academic year started, I had grown a lot in my confidence and was no longer as afraid of being found out.

My military career under DADT started off rather poorly. I entered basic training after a recent breakup which had—in conjunction with verbal taunting at school about my sexuality and a best friend who abandoned me once she found out I was gay—put me into a mild depression. I went in with a poor attitude, expecting my squadmates to find out about me just from my behavior and way of talking. I was upset with my life and didn't foresee it changing anytime soon. I knew I wouldn't be able to get help for my breakup, but I desperately wanted to talk with somebody about it.

I also knew that my personal life would be an inviolable subject for discussion for at least the next decade—I wouldn't be able to discuss personal problems (those that cause the most stress) with anyone until I got out of the military.

But then I decided to come out to my roommates, and some of my squadmates. All were very accepting and encouraging. Within that close group of friends, I suddenly found I could talk openly about my personal life, including the stresses of being gay in the military.

The next summer, I joined OutServe and met a whole hidden group of other lesbians and gays in the service. As the year went on, I felt more and more confident that DADT would soon be repealed and I became very open about my sexuality. I told my new roommates and most of my classmates; word got around, and I never had any problems with homophobia. Now that I was completely open with both myself and everyone else about who I was, I started dating again, and even soon came out of my yearlong depression.

Of course, I know that not everyone in the military is so accepting. Our training began not long after the repeal. During one training session a group of cadets sitting behind me made some disparaging remarks against gays and specifically gays in the military. For example: "It's so wrong to let that fag sex into this institution" and "They are wrong—it's a matter of religion and morals" and other numbing words to that effect. At the end of the briefing, as we were all departing, I recognized one of those cadets who had been sitting behind us. I talked to him later that night, explaining how disrespectful he had been and that, whatever his personal opinions, there was a proper forum for expressing his disagreement with policy but a training session was not one of them. He said it had mostly been his roommates making those remarks; although they had made him uncomfortable, he didn't have the courage to ask them to stop. But he said he really respected the fact that I'd confronted him and stood up for what was right. He also agreed he would now try to do a better job of defending gays and their new right to serve openly.

All in all, my life under "Don't Ask, Don't Tell" hasn't been terrible. On the contrary, I've had a much better time than some other service members who have been blackmailed and threatened because of their sexuality. The Air Force has been much more tolerant than I would have ever expected. And although I'm extremely happy that the policy is gone, I think it was a dead policy anyway. Now I'm just relieved that I can live my life openly without fearing discharge. And it's comforting to know that if I ever need real help for personal problems beyond the reach of my friends, I too can seek assistance.

Jeremy Johnson was an enlisted journalist
in the United States Navy from 1996 to 2007.
He is currently pursuing a degree in sociology
at the University of Maryland, Baltimore County.
He currently is seeking reenlistment into
the United States Navy.

I came out when I was eighteen and promptly joined the Navy. I served in the best way I knew how and grew up in uniform. I dedicated myself to the point that the Navy became my spouse. I couldn't live without it.

And yet it was making me miserable. "Don't Ask, Don't Tell" made me sacrifice things that I should have been pursuing that point in my life. My friends were slowly getting married and having kids and I wasn't even allowed to date, let alone have a partner or spouse.

So after ten years, I couldn't take the pressure any more and decided to write a coming-out letter to a very supportive commanding officer.

My decision to come out marked me as a quitter, the worst label within the military community. Advocates for the repeal of DADT wouldn't talk to me because I wasn't a victim of a witch hunt. I wasn't the victim of some clear misdeed. Despite being decorated, an enlisted leader, and well on my way to senior non-commissioned officer when I made that decision, I was looked at as a weak man who was seeking a way out. As a result, I became bitter and I shunned the DADT battle and the veteran label for more than two years.

And then something remarkable happened. A friend of mine, a straight veteran, connected me with an organization that was holding a conference in Los Angeles for millennial veterans. I didn't know what it was, but I took a chance and attended. It opened up my eyes to what I'd been missing—the real support wasn't to be found from fellow LGBT veterans, but from the straight allies I never knew I had when I wore the uniform.

That conference led to meeting a veteran's group locally in Baltimore and they invited me to become part of their small intimate family. We came together to do community service and that restored my faith in my own service. It was a healing experience.

I had always hoped to serve again, but I had all but given up on that dream. That changed in October 2010, when a court ruling was made that required the Department of Defense to stop enforcing DADT. Before I knew it, I was on the phone with a Navy reserve recruiter to see how long it would take to get back in uniform.

I also called the Air Force, the Army, the National Guard, and the active Navy. I was doing whatever I could to find an open spot in the military. The reception from the recruiters was less than welcoming. Most were happy to give me the screening, but few returned my phone calls afterward.

The Navy reserve recruiter was the most supportive. He encouraged me to gather up letters of endorsement to reenlist. I did. I actually received one letter of endorsement from the senior officer who discharged me in the first place, and a second from the head of our veterans group—an Iraq combat Marine veteran. But my reenlistment prospects kept changing—the courts ruled that gay troops could be accepted and then reversed the order and put DADT back in place a few days later. This flip-flop happened once more a few months later. The law on DADT seemed to change every day.

I look forward to the day when repeal is final and I can serve my country again in honor and with honesty about who I am.

Spencer Edwards is a second lieutenant in the
U.S. Air Force and a recent graduate of the
U.S. Air Force Academy.

I was raised in a family of fundamentalist Latter-day Saints, and grew up hearing my dad proclaim that homosexuals were an "abomination" who "chose their perverted lifestyle." When I hit puberty, I knew I was gay. At first I thought it was just a phase and it would pass, but soon I realized this was simply who I was. I decided I would be a good Mormon and live a celibate life.

Once I reached the conclusion I would always be attracted to other men, I couldn't keep it inside of me. I had to tell my mom. I felt like I was hiding part of myself and living dishonestly. I was sixteen when I told my mom I was gay. She told me she loved me, but she insisted on telling my father. Once my father found out, our relationship collapsed for a few years. Over time our ties have started to improve, but they are still very strained. Even though coming out to my mom seriously damaged my relationship with my father, it felt amazing to speak the truth.

I heard about the Air Force Academy the summer before my junior year of high school and thought it sounded interesting. Growing up, I'd never considered the military, but the more I thought about it the more it seemed like the right thing to do. In my mind the military was a place of perfect principle in which integrity, service, and honor were idolized. The first time I visited the academy, I noticed the honor code, cast in iron, embedded in a granite wall near the chapel: "We will not lie, steal, or cheat, nor tolerate among us anyone who does." I applied to the academy and was accepted.

Basic training was a blur. I was able to slip under the radar, and I got along well with my classmates. During basic training, you can never be alone; you must always be with a classmate. Every night I would wake up and have to use the restroom, and I would always wake up the same guy to go with me. My bathroom buddy, Jack*, changed my life forever and eventually helped me accept my sexuality.

I worked hard my first year and was very successful. After that first year my classmates and I were separated and sent to new squadrons. I remained close to Jack. As my sophomore year went on, I became very unhappy. My religion seemed more and more like a fairy tale—a fairy tale that was asking me, a gay man, to sacrifice a lot! Jack and I frequently talked about religion, and he helped me question the assumptions behind my beliefs. We eventually started talking about "Don't Ask, Don't Tell," and I began to suspect he was gay. Jack is an amazing guy, honest, kind, and honorable—everything I was taught a gay man was incapable of being. He made me realize that if I accepted being gay, I did not have to desert my values and I wouldn't suddenly become a radical. In May of my second year at the academy, I finally worked up my courage: I accepted I was gay and I broke away from the LDS church. My parents were furious at first, then very sad. When summer came I was swept away by training and didn't give DADT much thought.

The fall and winter of my junior year at the Air Force Academy was the worst time of my life. I met a guy in my squadron, Tom*. While dating Tom I began to feel the pressures of DADT. We had to keep our relationship a secret; consequently, I started to develop a hidden second life. While I was able to avoid straight-up lying, I was constantly misleading people: playing with my words and sneaking around. My life became inconsistent, deceptive, sometimes dishonest. Tom and I dated for a few months, but things eventually took a turn for the worse. I had a really difficult time handling our breakup. Because of "Don't Ask, Don't Tell," I was scared to talk to anyone about what was going on.

Jack was no longer at the academy when Tom and I broke up. My family couldn't help me—they either were unwilling to listen to me or believed my misery was a natural consequence of my "sinful ways." I was scared to talk to my friends, because I was afraid they would turn me in for being gay and I'd be kicked out. I was certain the counseling center and the chaplains would report me. As my depression got worse and worse, people noticed and started asking me more questions I couldn't answer honestly. I started feeling more and more dishonest. Once a month we would have an hour-long honor lesson in which we would talk about integrity. I remember on one very bad day listening to a discussion about how a life of integrity is a life without deception, one in which a person lives straightforwardly and has nothing to hide. I felt terrible. I wanted to hide my face and cry. Looking back, I don't know how I got through that semester.

After what felt like an eternity, the winter break finally arrived. I went to India on a cultural immersion trip. For several weeks I left behind my miserable double life at the academy under DADT, and I was able to start recovering. When I came back, I decided things had to change—I couldn't live the way I had the previous semester. I told a few people I trusted that I was gay and I isolated myself from those I couldn't tell. I joined wing staff to get away from Tom and the rest of my squadron. I came out to my new roommate, Ted.* Ted was very sympathetic to what I was going through and supported me whenever I was having a hard time. He remains one of the most considerate, open, hardworking people I have ever had the opportunity of meeting.

As the semester went on, things got a lot better. I made new friends, many of whom were also gay. We went to Denver almost every weekend. The emotional storm that had almost destroyed my life passed, and I healed. Eventually I realized I couldn't keep isolating myself from people. As a cadet, I was obligated to be involved in and contribute to the academy. I began reengaging my squadron and old friends.

Yet when I started getting more involved with people who couldn't know I was gay, the double life again emerged. I never quite had to lie outright, but I had to constantly come up with stories, hide things, and say things I did not believe. I thought a lot about integrity, and how I was sacrificing mine. Every day when I walked out of the academic building after class, I had to look at the iron-lettered honor code on the chapel wall. I listened to myself talking about honesty and integrity, knowing that every day I was betraying those values in myself. A person's integrity is his most valuable possession, worth any sacrifice to protect. The inherent dishonesty I was forced into under DADT was bothering me more and more, and again I started to slip into a depression. I finally decided I wouldn't live a life that forced me to sacrifice my integrity, no matter the cost. If "Don't Ask, Don't Tell" hadn't been repealed before the new Congress took over in January of 2011, I was going to turn myself in and get out of the military.

On December 18, when "Don't Ask, Don't Tell" was repealed, I was at my brother's wedding. I had been away from my computer for a few days, so I didn't know the Senate was voting on repeal that day. As we started taking wedding pictures, a friend texted me that the vote was taking place. In the middle of one picture,

I suddenly got four texts one right after another. I pulled out my phone and read that the Senate had repealed DADT! In an instant, I felt like the weight of the world had been lifted off my shoulders. It was a true once-in-a-lifetime moment.

Right after the picture was snapped, I told my mom the news. She was ecstatic and grabbed me in a big hug. It was amazing for me to know that even though she believes homosexuality is wrong, my mom loves and supports me.

Josh Engle is a staff sergeant in the U.S.
Air Force currently stationed at Tinker
Air Force Base, Oklahoma.

While stationed at Kadena Air Base in Okinawa, Japan, I had it all! The weather on the island was perfect year-round, the waters crystal clear, and I was excelling at my job. To make things even better, I met my first true love, a Marine named Greg.

As our relationship grew, I would pick him up off his base in the evenings and we would go out to dinner together. Eventually we got to the point where he would spend weekends with me in my room. Despite the restrictions we faced, we made it work.

Things became very difficult when Greg would go to sea for a couple months at a time. My father was in the Coast Guard, so I was used to having loved ones go away for a long time, but this was different. Everyone has seen the pictures of families standing on the piers, waving the ships off. I couldn't do that.

Deployment days were very emotional. The separation was

hard enough, but it was more difficult still because we knew we wouldn't have the same freedom of communication that others did.

When I drove Greg to the Navy base, I would take the back roads just to steal a few more minutes with him. Before we got to base, I would pull off the road to kiss him good-bye. We would sit and sigh, hug and kiss, knowing it would be our last time together for a while. And there was always that little sting of acknowledgment that we had to hide all this as well.

Once we were at port, I would help him lug all his gear and baggage down the pier and onto the ship. While everyone else was allowed to bring their spouses aboard, we had to pretend I was just another sailor or Marine coming across the brow. Luckily, as a Coast Guard kid I knew how to properly request permission to board a ship, and I made it look like I belonged there. All I had to do was use my thumb to cover up the part of my ID card with the Air Force emblem on it. Still, while on board I always feared I was going to get caught at any moment, ruining both of our careers.

After I left the ship, I would quietly slip off to the parking lot and leave while the rest of the families stayed behind, supporting one another and waving their heroes off. I would drive up to a hillside overlooking port and wave the ship off alone.

While the ship was under way, our communications were spotty and very unnatural. Everything that went on or off the ship was monitored, including e-mails and phone conversations. We would e-mail from work, but it was very generic and we couldn't use any endearing terms or talk too seriously. If I wanted to do any of that, I had a fake Yahoo account with a girl's name so he wouldn't draw any suspicion. Phone conversations were usually cold, but it was still nice to hear his voice. The only time we could ever freely be ourselves was when they were in port somewhere and Greg could use one of the satellite phones.

When his ship proudly paraded back into port, I would be there waiting. Of course, I couldn't be out waving and cheering for his return like the others, but I was just as excited and giddy to see my love. To avoid any unwanted attention, I would park somewhere on the base and wait for him to call so that I could quickly pick him up. Then we'd go to the same spot off the road where we'd said our good-byes, finally able to give each other the loving embrace we'd both been waiting for.

Through these times, we have made a difficult situation work, proving that love can conquer all. Both of us, however, felt we were second-class citizens and we struggled with having to constantly hide. I look forward to the day when any two people in love can live out in the open and show their love freely, just like any other couple out there on the pier.

Steven Butler* is first lieutenant in the U.S. Air Force. A 2008 graduate of the U.S. Air Force Academy, he currently works for Africa Command.

I n the fall of 2008, I arrived at Maxwell Air Force Base, Alabama, for my first formal training as a commissioned second lieutenant.

I was ecstatic to finally put my four years of leadership knowledge I had learned at the Air Force Academy into practice. The Air and Space Basic Course, or ASBC as we usually call it, is a young commissioned officer's first introduction into the military. It is a six-week course involving team building exercises, crisis management scenarios, physical fitness tests, and professional growth. For the first five weeks, students sit through professional military development classes that touch on everything from the deployment cycle to the structure of every military branch. Since I had graduated from the Air Force Academy, much of the training was a bit repetitive and I found myself teaching others and helping them through the course. It would be safe to say that, in those first five weeks, I stood out as someone with clear leadership potential. I was confident; all the training I had been put through had helped me overcome my doubts about being a gay man in the military. If I could excel at this, I started to believe, then maybe there really was a place for me in this "long blue line" of military officers.

In our final week of ASBC, all the new officers were partnered with senior enlisted officers at the Senior Noncommissioned Officer Academy across town. The purpose of this week was to expose us to enlisted personnel and learn how to behave as officers. There were two particular SNCOs who really took me under their wing. Not only were they exceptional people, but their knowledge and military discipline were strengths that I aspired to. Whether it was instructing me on how to write the best evaluation for my future "troop" or advising me on how to mentor troubled airmen, these men took the time to help guide me.

The last day of our time together we played a game that threw us into different situations and forced us to take opinions on hard issues. First they made us stand in the middle of the room. The instructor explained to us that each corner of the room represented a stance on each issue. One corner was "Completely agree." The second, "Agree with reservations." The third was "Disagree with reservations." And finally, "Completely disagree." As we began this exercise, key hot topics came up on a projection screen, such as abortion, treatment of prisoners of war, and minorities in the workplace. I stood strong in the liberal corner, arguing for abortion rights, fair treatment of POWs, and protecting minority rights in the workplace. Among the others in the classroom there was a very typical social spread on these issues. However, a majority of the senior enlisted officers took more conservative stances. The two senior enlisteds who I'd become close to that week were the exception—they stood next to me on most of the issues.

The last slide that popped up on the screen was "Repeal of Don't Ask, Don't Tell." I was completely caught off guard. In that moment, the wind was swiftly knocked out of my sails. I began to turn red. I was completely unprepared to face this question in front of the class. *What do I do?* I thought to myself, panicked. *Are people going to judge me? Will everyone automatically assume that I'm gay and get me in trouble?* All the confidence I had gained in the past six weeks was right then a distant memory as the members of my discussion group began shuffling around the room to get to their respective corners. Shaking and feeling as though I was suffocating, I began walking toward the "Completely agree" corner. *I'm a gay man,* I thought to myself. *Of course I need to be in that corner.* But the feelings of doubt and worry about being scrutinized by my peers stopped me in my tracks. I ultimately found myself standing in the "Agree with reservations" corner. I forced myself behind a few others, too embarrassed to even look around the room. I cannot recall a word of what anyone in that classroom said, other than the two men I had spent the previous four days with.

How would my mentors respond? As I looked around the

room, I saw that they'd sided with the "Completely disagree" faction. One of them said he believed homosexuality to be a choice and that the military was no place for "those kinds of people." The other referenced a shower scenario, saying that he "didn't want a gay man looking at me in the shower." As the instructor came to my corner, I looked toward the ground, hoping I wouldn't be called on to defend my position. The proctor, maybe sensing my discomfort, asked me to state my case. Stuttering and stumbling, I stood there and said to the class, "I believe the military would have to work out certain issues such as gay men and women showering on the front lines before it could be fully implemented." In that moment, I would have said anything to simply finish the discussion and leave the room.

Immediately following the roundtable we broke for lunch. I rushed out of the classroom fighting back tears. I went back to my room and completely broke down. Every bit of insecurity I had about being a gay man rose up inside of me in that hotel room. I sobbed at the thought that my two mentors—officers I had respected and seen as my allies—believed me to be unfit to serve. Hadn't I proved myself? An academy graduate, a leader in my flight—what was wrong with me? But most of all, my anger and pain were directed at myself. I had stood there in fear of the "Don't Ask, Don't Tell" policy and couldn't even stand up for the person I was. I allowed a discussion about gays in the service to take place and yet I couldn't even muster up the courage to explain to others why they were wrong. I even reinforced their ideas by conceding their absurd shower scenario when I knew in my heart that this was just not true. I lay on the floor defeated for the entire lunch period, but as I picked myself up I thought to myself, *One day I'll show them.* I washed off my face and walked out the door. The next week I graduated at the top of my flight.

Carlos Coronado is a captain in the U.S. Air Force,
currently stationed at Buechel Air Base, Germany.

When we first founded OutServe Germany, we struggled to figure out how to build the community. The chapters were created so that service members could more easily reach out and find each other, but the online forum was silent. Finally, someone suggested we organize outings, meet-ups in random cities just to get together as a group and do some sightseeing. As it happened, our first trip, to Frankfurt, would take place on December 18, 2010—the day the Senate was to vote on "Don't Ask, Don't Tell."

We first met in the lobby of the Le Méridien hotel. I was greeted by a couple of the guys and girls, quietly listening on their iPhones to a C-SPAN feed from the Senate floor. The mood was anxious but hopeful as we set out for the Christmas markets in the center square of Frankfurt. We sipped on glühwein as we finally got to know one another in person.

After the markets we gathered in an Australian pub for dinner.

We sat and ordered food and drinks while we listened to the floor debate on the DADT repeal. When John McCain took to the floor, one of us shouted, "Goddamn it, that old fart won't shut up!" As we were enjoying our meal, the vote began at last. It felt like we were counting down to New Year's.

When the final tally came and repeal had passed, we all screamed and toasted. I immediately started calling my friends. One of them, stationed in Naples, Italy, hadn't been paying attention to the news, so he was floored when I told him, "We won!" I then called a girl I knew in Germany who was beginning to despair about staying in the service under "Don't Ask, Don't Tell." She broke into sobs when I passed along the news. As we were leaving the restaurant, I called a member in the OutServe UK group; he and his chapter were already celebrating in London.

All around the world, service members were toasting the end of "Don't Ask, Don't Tell." We were all connected by OutServe, and by our hopes for a brighter future. I can think of no happier start for our organization.

Jacob Light* is in the U.S. Marine Corps.
This story originally appeared in the first
print edition of OutServe **Magazine.**

My wife is home with our two beautiful, healthy children. We live in base housing and also own a home in the South with a tenant who pays the rent on time and takes good care of our house. Our only debt is good debt: a mortgage, student loans, and one car payment. At work, I command a Marine rifle company. My company has 187 infantry Marines who are well trained, well prepared, and ready to fight for their country and their corps. I regularly think of committing suicide.

I realized I was gay in high school, though upon closer reflection, the writing was on the wall long before that. To say I was in denial is an understatement. It did not help that my mother, an evangelical convert late in life, realized my sexual leanings and ordered me to counseling with her minister. They both managed to convince me (at the time a struggling recent evangelical convert myself) that my relationship with boys was unnatural, ungodly, and would ensure I had a reservation in hell when I died. Naturally, I believed them.

At college, I did what my family expected me to do. I went to a big, conservative school with a large ROTC program, I suppressed my sexuality publically, and I went about my life. My long-term girlfriend broke up with me during my sophomore year after my secret long-term ex-boyfriend called her and told her about our relationship. I didn't date anyone after that for about three years.

Fast-forward to college graduation and commissioning. I started dating a girl at the end of college, and proposed to her shortly before starting the Marines' Basic Officer Course in Quantico, Virginia. The suggestion to propose had come from my best friend. He didn't know I was gay, and I was too scared and too deep in the closet to tell him. I bought a ring, she said yes, and we were married five months later. At this point, there was absolutely no doubt in my mind that I was gay, but there was also no chance that I would ever consider coming out to anyone, so I assumed I could simply change my feelings over time, and that I would eventually become straight—or at least bisexual.

After my first deployment, my wife and I decided to try and get pregnant. I realize I should have told her before this point about my sexuality, but I was too ashamed, and I wanted to have a child before my next deployment. I had long concluded that my life would be one of silence and suppression of my feelings—the safest and most considerate thing to do. We were immediately successful, and my wife became pregnant with our twins. I deployed a few weeks later. Following the second deployment, I returned home to my new family. When I left, I had a wife and a dog. When I returned, I had a full house. Becoming a father was the best experience of my life.

But being a father, especially as my kids grew older and smarter, has made me realize the importance of honesty with my children. What would they think if they were to discover my sexuality when they were teenagers or adults? Would they hate me for lying to them and their mom? Would they resent me because I was not honest with them? And about my wife—how much longer could I make her unwittingly suffer without the knowledge of my true feelings and desires? How much longer would I let her think that my lack of desire for her was her fault, or that she was somehow unattractive? I knew that the longer I waited, the more painful the truth would be.

When I was at PME (professional military education) school, two significant issues began to creep into my conscience. First, I realized that my true political beliefs no longer matched those I professed. Despite being raised in conservative south Texas, attending a very conservative university, and serving as an officer in the most conservative of our nation's armed services, I was actually quite liberal. While most people have this revelation in college, I waited until I was almost thirty before allowing myself to admit it. At the same time, I also began questioning my religion and faith.

These two revelations, both life-changing for me in their own way, were perhaps the most significant contributing factors to my ultimate decision to come out to my wife. Once I was able to accept myself spiritually and politically, my mind and heart were freed to accept who I truly was. Armed with the power of that knowledge, I decided that I would tell my wife the truth, and I would do so before the year's end.

I came out to my wife just before my next deployment. I feared that if she discovered my desires on her own, she would never be able to forgive me, and I knew that her eventual forgiveness was critical to my long-term emotional stability. I knew that my desire for men went far beyond sex; it was the relationship I wanted—and that demanded a total lifestyle change.

It was a Wednesday in October when I made the decision. I called her from work and asked her if she could have a friend watch the kids one night later in the week—we needed to talk. She immediately suspected something was wrong. By the time I arrived home, she was very distraught. She kept asking me questions, trying to pry the subject of the conversation out. I wouldn't tell her, and that made it worse. I had hoped for a Friday night talk, so we could have the weekend to work through the intense emotions I knew would follow, but she couldn't wait. I eventually quit stalling. We sent the kids to a neighbor's house, sat down on the couch, and I spilled my guts. At first, she just sat there, shaking violently, barely able to catch her breath. She kept saying, "Okay, okay, okay,

okay," as if she could somehow talk herself into accepting the complete destruction of the world she knew by wishing everything to be okay. But it wasn't okay. We talked and cried for four hours that first night. She desperately needed someone to talk to, and so she asked if she could call her mother. I told her that was fine, and she made me promise to stay in the room. In spite of her anger and disbelief, she wanted me to hear every word she said, because she wanted me to know that she wasn't going to run to her family with the kids. She was at the lowest point of her entire life, but she wanted to be sure that I knew something: this was still *our* family, and we had to handle this as a team.

It was hard that night; it still is. But it was the right thing to do. While she is still hurt and angry, she does not hate me because I am gay. She is angry because I lied to her. We've agreed to stay together for a time until we work out what is best for the kids. We've decided to get divorced, but not rush into it. She's even let me start seeing a guy I really like, a fellow service member who I can see myself committed to for a long time. So, there is hope for progress.

So why do I think about suicide? Because the world I built for myself is crumbling around me. Despite the repeal of "Don't Ask, Don't Tell," I'm terrified of my Marines finding out that I am gay. I'm terrified of telling my parents. I'm terrified that my wife and I will fight about our kids and she will take them somewhere that I won't be able to get stationed. Life is so much better for our generation than it has been for previous ones. I'm grateful every day for those who have paved the way for our society to recognize LGBT people as equals, but I struggle every day with the reality of living on the threshold of this new world. My kids, my Marines, and the hope for a future with someone I can love openly are the only reasons I'm still alive today.

Joshua Hawley is a lieutenant colonel and
Army physician at Tripler Army Medical Center
in Honolulu. He specializes in infectious
diseases and internal medicine.

I am an Army doctor. During my first assignment, at Fort Lewis, Washington, I learned firsthand how the Army can become your second family, despite DADT and against all odds. Something happened to me that was both terrible and transformative, and in the aftermath I realized that my Army colleagues saw me as a human being, a friend, and a valuable team member, and not merely as a gay man who does not belong in a heterosexual military.

I grew up in an Army family, and I always dreamed of wearing the uniform myself, like my father and my grandfather before me. I grew up in Virginia, and I started medical school there on an Army scholarship before I ever admitted to myself that I was gay. I finally came out to my friends and family during my last two years of medical school. Although my family was generally supportive, my mother was worried that my career would be destroyed if anyone I worked with found out I was gay. Her concerns, in my case, were unfounded: my Army experience has only confirmed that the military will successfully adapt to open service by gays and lesbians.

After graduation from medical school, I moved to Fort Lewis, near Seattle, to begin residency training in internal medicine. It was a big move for me: it was both my first Army assignment and my first time living far across the country from my family. I needed to find a new support system, and I quickly found it in my new residency classmates. A medical residency is a difficult, scary, and stressful time, but it is also a bonding experience for those who go through it together. It was not long before I told one of my classmates, who was also a housemate, that I was gay. I was moved to tell her because I had begun dating another Fort Lewis Army officer, named Trevor*. I didn't want to keep a secret in my own home. Trevor moved to a new duty station after my first year of residency, and our relationship ended. But he provided the impetus for me to begin coming out to my residency classmates. By the end of my second year in training, all of my colleagues knew I was gay. I did not have any negative reactions from any of them, but I was still afraid of what might happen if my chain of command found out.

During my third and final year of residency, I met my future husband, Johnathon. Although we are both health care professionals and were both members of the same large Seattle running club, we had never met until we happened to be at the same bar one evening. We began a whirlwind romance, which was made all the more urgent by my impending PCS move to Alaska. He agreed to make the move north with me after only six months of dating, and so we began to plan our new life together.

Just a month before we were to board our Alaska-bound ferry, Johnathon joined some friends for a weekend trip to Bellingham to participate in the Ski to Sea multisport relay race. I was working, so I had to stay home. After a long night shift, I was asleep in my bedroom when I was awakened by a flashlight shining in my eyes. I was groggy, so it took me a few seconds to realize there was a masked intruder in my bedroom with a knife. I jumped out of bed and attempted to escape past him out the door, but he blocked my path and stabbed me twice in the abdomen. I thought he would kill me, but after tying me up and further assaulting me, he departed, leaving me bloodied and bound. I waited a long time, listening to make sure he was gone, before working my way out of my bonds and calling 911. The police never made an arrest, and the identity and motivation of my attacker are still a mystery. The next thing I remember is waking up in a Seattle hospital the next day, after having abdominal surgery to repair two liver lacerations.

This is when my traumatic experience unexpectedly became one of liberation. With my parents on their way from the East Coast, Johnathon and my Army colleagues rallied around me to help me recover. Over the next three days, every single one of my residency classmates traveled an hour from Fort Lewis to downtown Seattle to wish me well—some multiple times. They brought me get-well cards, flowers, books, and Alaska travel guides. Even my chain of command, including both my immediate supervisor and his supervisor, came to visit me. They met my boyfriend in the hospital room, and they went to great lengths to reassure me that my sexual orientation made no difference to them. Although it did not hit me right away in my narcotic-induced fog, I realized later that a great burden had been lifted when I no longer had to worry about keeping my secret.

Although I had to retread this long coming-out road with each subsequent PCS move to a new duty station, my experience at Fort Lewis taught me that there is always a supportive Army family, even under "Don't Ask, Don't Tell." I learned to expect acceptance rather than rejection, and I began to carry myself with a new confidence in my professional and personal life. Although my positive experience was different from the discrimination suffered by many other gay and lesbian service members, I believe it is an important story to tell during the repeal of DADT, especially in light of the dire predictions by antigay organizations and politicians.

With the support of Johnathon, my family, and my Army family, I completely recovered from my injuries and we made our move to Fairbanks, where I encountered another welcoming Army family. We have since moved to different stations together two more times, and our relationship has survived the frequent trainings, temporary duty assignments, and deployments that punctuate a military family's life.

After ten years together, Johnathon and I will be married in Washington, D.C., later this year. Although he will not receive spousal benefits from the Army due to the Defense of Marriage Act, we are excited to finally gain legal recognition of our relationship without fear of career repercussions for me. And our birth families and our Army family will all be there to celebrate with us at our wedding!

Todd Burton is a lieutenant colonel in the Army National Guard. He is an Active Guard and Reserve officer assigned to the National Guard Bureau in Washington, D.C., and a coleader of the Washington, D.C., OutServe.

In 1989, I completed ROTC and was commissioned a year before I graduated. I was also just starting to explore what it meant to be gay. Open military service by gays and lesbians was beginning to bubble-up on college campuses and I was active as a student leader, so these two separate worlds were bound to intersect. Several friends in the university senate initiated a resolution that proposed to ban ROTC from campus until the restrictions were rescinded. I timidly stood with the sponsors and seconded the motion, although it was ultimately not successful.

After graduation, I began to come out and to get involved in the gay community. I expanded my circle of gay friends, became involved in an Episcopal church with a large gay membership, began coming out to my friends and select family members, got involved in my first relationship, and even did a stint as a part-time bartender in the local gay watering hole. I was able to keep my personal life separate from the military and I continued to attend training and work my way up through the ranks.

One of my mentors at the time was a retired Air Force colonel who was active in my church and who appeared in uniform on the cover of *Gay Chicago* magazine during the height of the debates that led to enactment of DADT. Frank taught me that it was possible to effectively juggle these seemingly disparate aspects of my life—but he also warned me about the potential for damage to self-worth and personal dignity.

In 1993 I attended the March on Washington for Lesbian, Gay and Bi Equal Rights and Liberation. This was an amazing time as Bill Clinton had swept into office with a promise to end the ban on open military service. It was this event that galvanized a changing perspective on my sexual orientation. I was surrounded by hundreds of thousands of people just like me, and I came to realize that being gay was not something to be ashamed of. I became more involved, eventually moving to the "boystown" area in Chicago and participating more fully in the community there.

But I was still drilling with the Illinois Guard and my hopes were dashed as Clinton capitulated to military leadership and a reluctant Congress. I debated whether to continue with my dual life or to move on from service. Then the military threw me a curve ball. I was asked to take a short tour in the Pentagon to work a special project. I agreed, moved to Washington, and went to work four-teen to sixteen hours a day for the next couple of years. I was back in the closet, but working on important issues and supporting the most senior leadership in the building. It was exciting, interesting, and fulfilling work so I jumped at the opportunity when they of-fered to make the assignment permanent, knowing full well that it meant a long-term stint back in the closet.

I don't regret this decision. My military career is rewarding. I get to serve with some of the best and brightest men and women in this country—true heroes who put on the uniform every morning and commit to protecting our nation and the values we hold dear. I have the opportunity to work on important issues and know that what I am doing directly impacts the men and women serving in harm's way.

But with the rewards of military service comes great personal sacrifice. Camaraderie is an important aspect of military service, yet I find myself separated from my peers. I don't socialize after work with military types and I avoid developing the close personal connections between soldiers serving together—there are just too many opportunities to slip and disclose my sexual orientation. I haven't yet found it possible to reconcile my career with a relation-ship, and my involvement in the gay community has faded as I in-creasingly immerse myself in the details of my duties.

I could easily continue on this path and finish out my career in silence, very possibly earning another promotion and increased responsibility. But the repeal of DADT allows me the opportunity to reconcile two competing aspects of my life. I owe it to myself to finish out my career honestly and with dignity. I also owe it to my fellow LGBT service members to act as a role model for successful service after repeal.

I have no doubt that this decision may have negative repercussions. I might not get that next promotion and could easily be shunted off into some backwater assignment. But I have a great deal of faith in my leaders. They are great Americans, committed to well and faithfully discharging the duties of the office in which they serve. I believe that they will seek out the best, most qualified soldier without regard to sexual orientation. I intend to be that soldier.

The following interview was conducted with Jeff and Lori Wilfahrt, father and mother of Corporal Andrew Wilfahrt, who was killed in action in 2011, two months after the repeal of "Don't Ask, Don't Tell." The interview appeared in a video produced by Courage Campaign and OutServe and was released on YouTube.

JEFF: Our son Andrew was a gay man, very openly gay and loud and proud about it while he lived here in Minneapolis. Of course, when he went into the military, he had to go back into the closet.

LORI: He was a very peaceful person in many regards, and the stories from people in his unit say he kept people calm when things got rough.

JEFF: He ended up being the guidon bearer in his platoon. He got that honor for being the most physically fit man in the platoon. As I understand it, his physical fitness score was 300. His commander was curious what the hell Andrew Wilfahrt was doing in the Army. His aptitude tests were off the charts. I guess the commander couldn't quite understand what a man like that wanted to be a grunt for. The entire platoon became indebted to him as a friend and a confidant, a support.

LORI: People in his unit knew that he was gay, the wives knew, the girlfriends knew—people knew, and nobody cared. He proved himself first that he was a hard worker and he was a loyal friend, and he was going to take care of them when he could and when he needed to. The other part just didn't matter.

JEFF: Being gay was the least interesting thing about him. He was a soldier's soldier—all of his commanding officers were struck by him. He was good to the people around him. The Army should be thankful they got him, and I think they are. They have certainly expressed it to this family.

To persist with this bias, this prejudice—whatever the basis may be—is a foolish thing. There is no gain.

Andrew thought he'd go, so that somebody else with family and children didn't have to go. Sergeant Williams, the other man that was wounded when Andrew was killed, is a family man. He was the sergeant commander of the vehicle. He has a couple of kids. He's doing well, he's healing. We have recently seen a photograph of him in his hospital bed with his kids there, and they all got big grins. So I guess Andrew got what he wanted. It's become pretty evident that Andrew's body shielded and protected Sergeant Williams from blast he took.

The next thing I want to say is that the Army has been very good to this family. They have treated us well. They have been respectful and they have been there for us, and I really do appreciate it. They took us to Dover for the return of his remains. That was very stirring, to the root of our souls—to stand there in the driving rain . . .

Soldiers don't die for our freedom of speech, they don't die for patriotism, they don't die for noble causes, they don't die for our political agendas. Soldiers die for each other. If the man, or woman, to your right or left is doing their job, then that's all that matters. Gender, race, creed, sexuality just aren't on their radar. Can they shoot straight? Can they take care of each other? Do they have your back? That's all a soldier cares about.

ACKNOWLEDGMENTS

The true heroes of this book are the military members who shared their stories. Thank you for your contributions and your bravery. Thank you first and foremost to Lindsay Whalen, my editor at The Penguin Press, who always knew how to keep me on track—you are truly amazing.

Thank you to literary agent extraordinaire, David Kuhn, who helped me toward the idea for *Our Time* and who found a great home for the book with The Penguin Press. Ann Godoff believed in this book and made it a reality. Thank you also to my publicity team, Penguin Press publicity director Sarah Hutson and publicist Suzanne Williams. Production editor Noirin Lucas and copyeditor Nicholas LoVecchio were able to work on a very tight deadline to bring this book to readers.

This book wouldn't have been possible without the membership of OutServe. We couldn't have built OutServe without you. Tom Carpenter and Zoe Dunning were the first to believe in Out-Serve, and I can never repay you two. Aaron Belkin and Christopher Neff at the Palm Center, you are amazing individuals and were essential to building our organization. Cathy Renna, we have you to thank for running our first public relations for the organization.

Special thanks to the board of OutServe who have worked so hard in growing this organization: Sue Fulton, Katie Miller, and Jonathan Hopkins. There are so many people in this movement who took the time to help me on this journey: Rick Jacobs, Trevor Thomas, Dan Choi, Emily Sussman, Fred Sainz, Brian Bond, Aubrey Sarvis, Gautam Raghavan, Tobias Barrington Wolff, Ben Mishkin, Robin McGehee, Justin Elzie, Heather Cronk, Clarke Cooper, and Mya Lake Reyes. Aaron Tax, my lawyer at SLDN, was a rock as I was going through my own troubles under "Don't Ask, Don't Tell."

The media was so important to the growth of OutServe; thank you to all who gave me the opportunity to share our story: Rachel Maddow, Don Lemon, Andrew Harmon, Chris Geidner, Chris Johnson, Ed O'Keefe, Leo Shane, Mike O'Reiley, Pam Spaulding, Andy Towle, Joe Sudbay, John Aravosis, Andrea Stone, Lisa Leff, Mike Signorile, Phil Reese, Adam Polaski, Karen Ocamb, and every media outlet that gave gay and lesbian troops a voice.

I want to thank my personal friends who have helped me on

this journey: Kevin Calderwood, who started the website when this idea first launched, Emily Sheldon, Adam Kretz, Ryan Quinn, Scott Konzem, A. J. Jenkins, Kevin Minch, Glenn Prince, Matt Stannard, Kristen Owen, Matt Rose, Jameson Lamie, Scott Weaver, Randy Chlebek, Katie Thomas, and Karl Johnson. Thank you to my family for being so supportive of this project.

Most important, thank you to all the people who worked tirelessly, even sacrificing their careers, to end the ban on gays serving in the military.

I'm saving my most important acknowledgment for last. Ty Walrod, none of this would have been possible without you. You have truly been my best friend over the past two years as we worked to establish OutServe and I look forward to seeing what we can do next.

ABOUT THE AUTHOR

Active duty Air Force officer Josh Seefried is a co-founder and codirector of OutServe, the association of LGBT actively serving military personnel. He graduated from the U.S. Air Force Academy in 2009.